The Fading of the
Maoist Vision

The Fading of the Maoist Vision:

City and Country in China's Development

RHOADS MURPHEY

 *METHUEN*

NEW YORK   LONDON   TORONTO

Library of Congress Cataloging in Publication Data

Murphey, Rhoads
  The fading of the Maoist vision.

  Bibliography: p.
  Includes index.
  1. Urban policy—China.   2. Urbanization—China.
3. China—Social conditions.   4. Urban policy—
India.   5. India—Social conditions.   I. Title.
HT147.C48M87   1980   306.7'6'0951   80-10115
ISBN 0-416-60201-0

Manufactured in the United States of America
First American edition

Published in the United States of America by
Methuen, Inc.
733 Third Avenue
New York, N.Y. 10017

Published in Canada by
Methuen Publications
2330 Midland Avenue
Agincourt, Ontario M1S 1P7

Published in all other countries by
Methuen & Co Ltd
11 New Fetter Lane
London EC4P 4EE

For Ted, who encouraged me to write
this book, perhaps too patiently.

et ventus serenus ad portum incolumem

Table of Contents

Maps, Plates, and Table

Foreword

THIS BOOK IS THE RESULT OF A GOOD MANY YEARS OF READING, thinking, observation, and writing about the problems of development and the urban-rural spectrum, particularly in Asia, where I have spent several periods of my adult life but which has also been the consistent focus of my work. The present study was finished immediately after a year of residence and travel in Asia in 1978–79, by VW bus from Europe through the Middle East and India, on through Southeast Asia, and thence to China and Japan. About two months of this time was spent travelling in India, mainly in rural areas and small towns but punctuated by visits to most of the major cities, including conversations with a great variety of planners, officials, scholars, and others. This period in India, during which I visited nearly every state and most districts, was followed shortly by a more circumscribed and briefer return visit to China, but there too, as on previous visits, I had the opportunity to see both rural and urban areas in some detail. I lived and worked in China from 1942 to 1946 as a member of an international medical relief group, which gave me among other things a familiarity with the traditional base against which to compare what has been accomplished since. Earlier and later work and residence in India, including some two years during the mid-1950's and shorter visits thereafter, have built up a degree of familiarity with the Indian scene as well. A good many of the statements in this book are based on my own observations of rural and urban China and India, or on those of friends and colleagues as reported to me informally.

I have also tried to study both Chinese and Indian ideas and performances in the field of urban planning and rural development through following what they and others have published about such matters, and have myself produced several published studies (listed in the bibliography at the end of this book) where I have pursued many of the themes dealt with here in greater detail. What I attempt in this book is a broader overview and an evaluation, after some thirty years of determined efforts at change in revolutionary China and independent India. I leave to the readers to draw whatever conclusions they choose from the apparent coincidence of a genuine political democracy with an at least respectable progress in economic development in India, and from the seemingly similar overall rate and level of development under a very different political system in China. The Chinese themselves now give one the impression that they do not regard a degree of free expression and activity as incompatible with economic growth, perhaps even that they see a positive and causal correlation between the two.

The romanization of Chinese words presents a difficult problem, made more so by the recent increase in the use of the officially approved pinyin system, since 1978 standard for all Chinese government publications in Western languages and consequently widely used in the Western press. This new system is largely, but not entirely, phonetic: it uses a number of letters and combinations which differ sharply from the system previously in most common use in both China and abroad, known as Wade-Giles. Unfortunately, many readers will be accustomed to the Wade-Giles spellings, especially for common place and personal names, and will find the pinyin spellings strange or even incomprehensible. As an unsatisfactory but perhaps best compromise, I have given pinyin versions of all proper names in italics and in brackets at the point of first use, and in each appropriate index entry, but have otherwise retained the earlier conventional spellings, on grounds of familiarity to most readers. Pre-1949 spellings or alternative names are occasionally given and appear unitalicized in brackets after some proper names.

The bulk of this book was written during a sabbatical leave from the University of Michigan, to whom it is a pleasure to express my thanks for their support as well as to the Horace Rackham School of Graduate Studies for a grant-in-aid during the same period. Much of the writing was accomplished while I was in Japan as a Fellow of the Japan Society for the Promotion of Science and a Visiting Professor at Tokyo University. I am grateful to the J.S.P.S. for making this possible, and especially to Professor Iwao Kobori, my host at Tokyo University, who made my stay in Japan maximally pleasant and rewarding as well as fruitful. James Sheridan and James Chan each gave the complete manuscript a careful critical reading and I am indebted to both of them for valuable suggestions. Judith Siegel has done a superb job with the maps, and equally important, done so with expedition and good humor. Finally, I welcome the chance to thank John von Knorring of Methuen for his cheerful and effective help and for making the usually frustrating process of turning a manuscript into a book a genuine pleasure.

Ann Arbor
October, 1979

The Fading of the
Maoist Vision

1. Cities and the Developing World

THE CITY HAS BEEN THE FOCUS OF HUMAN DEVELOPMENT FOR some six thousand years. Indeed the word city comes from the same root as "civilization" — a Western-centered derivation but not inappropriate to the experience of the rest of the world. Cities everywhere, however different from the Western model in form and function, have played both a symbolic and an enabling or presiding role as pinnacles of human achievement and as centers of innovation.

With the coming of industrialization, the city has acquired a new character, one which has increasingly been seen as creating at least as many problems as it solves. It is not difficult to see the modern industrial city as a mistake, a wrong turn which has failed to produce a net improvement in total human welfare or which has instead become a new monster. Most modern cities are easily perceived as dreary, grey wastelands housing dreary, grey, de-humanized people working as cogs in a machine which seems to destroy much of what is good about life, especially by contrast with rural areas. Industrial cities blight the natural environment and their pollution further damages the quality of human life. They also breed tension, violence, callousness, selfishness, corruption, moral degeneration, artificiality, and what is often called "anomie", a loss of meaning in human interrelations which may well lie at the root of most urban problems. The modern industrial city may produce new material wealth, but perhaps at the cost of the human soul.

Such a perspective is especially understandable in the so-called "developing" world, pre-disposed to be critical (as well as envious) of the character and accomplishments of the industrialized world, eager for the wealth and power which industrialization can bring but unwilling to become merely a second-class echo which reproduces all the mistakes of the flawed original. It should be possible for later comers to design a better path to the fruits of industrialization, and to build cities which enhance rather than erode human welfare. The end of colonialism in the ashes of the Second World War yielded to new independent governments in much of the developing world, in an atmosphere of hope and of new nationalist visions of a better future. In China, a revolution of unprecedented scale and depth came to power determined to re-make the country and to chart for the Chinese fifth of mankind a radical new course to wealth and power.

What happens in the developing world, and especially in its efforts to combat poverty through industrialization, is of overriding importance: by the end of the present century—less than twenty years from now—it will contain about four fifths of the world's people. Most of them will probably still be village-based farmers, but the efforts toward industrialization, now still largely confined to the big cities, will surely continue. Can these efforts succeed in raising mass welfare safely beyond the margins of poverty? In particular, will increased industrial output yield better living conditions for most people, village farmers and urban workers? Can the developing world devise new solutions to the problems which urban-centered industrialization has created in the "developed" world? Or can it follow a different path, one which minimizes the destructive aspects of urban over-concentration in terms of both material and spiritual welfare and which uses industrial technology to serve real human needs? In most of these new nations, especially those with a recent history of colonialism, such a goal is widely discussed, and in many specifically planned for. In Chairman Mao's words, "*People* are the most precious things", not GNP; development should make life better for them, not worsen it.

The pattern so far, in the second half of the twentieth century, does not suggest a great deal of optimism. It is true that in most of the developing world there has been a slow, and still small, rise in average living standards since 1950, due primarily to increasing industrialization and its consequences in improved medical and public health care, better and cheaper transport (so that famine is less common), and new inputs to the agricultural sector: fertilizers, irrigation equipment, improved crop strains, pesticides, and some machines. But these gains, still relatively small and jeopardized by the rapid population growth they have enabled, have been won for the most part from a development pattern which replicates the earlier Western-Soviet-Japanese experience: a few huge cities, dangerously overcrowded and polluted, and a far vaster rural countryside where most peoples' lives are as yet only little affected. The gap between city and countryside, in material welfare and in quality of life, has not been reduced by growing industrialization, but widened. The new wealth generated by industrialization is overwhelmingly concentrated in the cities, where it supports urban and cosmopolitan lifestyles totally alien to the rural hinterlands.

The great majority of urbanites however live under miserable conditions, once familiar in Western cities at a similar early stage of industrialization but now conveniently forgotten. In the typical big city of the developing world now, most people live without a piped water supply and depend on access to a public tap shared with hundreds of others, inadequate in amount and usually unfit for drinking. As much as a quarter, often more, of the urban population lives in squatter shacks—which even so may be preferable to the hopelessly overcrowded and miserable tenements which shelter most of the rest, apart from the many who have no homes and sleep in the streets, under bridges, or in railway and bus stations. As much as the third (more in some cities) are unemployed or "disguised" unemployed—usually a euphemism for beggars and panhandlers in various forms. Virtually no medical facilities are available for most of these people, and only about a third of those of school age manage to obtain the equivalent of primary schooling.[1]

If living conditions in the cities are so dreadful, and employment so inadequate, why do they continue to grow, as they do? The answer is clearly that the villages are seen by most people, if not as no better, then as offering too little opportunity for change and for upward mobility. New economic opportunity is concentrated in the cities, most of all and most varied in the largest cities. There is not enough to go around among all of those who seek it but, despite the risks, the prospect is more attractive for many people than remaining in what they see as a dead end in the villages. While there has been in most areas some absolute improvement in village living standards, economic growth has been far greater in the cities and it is also there that new kinds of careers can be pursued leading upward in status as well as in material rewards, away from the hard and limited life of the peasants. This is of course the same process by which cities grew so rapidly in the course of the commercial and industrial revolutions in the West and Japan. Then, as in the developing world now, cities grew more on the basis of migration from the countryside than as a result of natural increase on the part of the urban population itself. Yet eighteenth and early nineteenth century London, or later nineteenth century New York or Chicago, almost certainly contained as large a share of wretchedly poor people, and under equally miserable conditions, as contemporary cities in the developing world; the death rate was probably higher, health and education facilities even more limited, and working conditions in factories and sweat shops far worse.

Here are some descriptions of workers' life in England in the 1830's:

> The houses [are] filthy, unfurnished, deprived of all the accessories to decency and comfort . . . [They] are ill-drained, ill-ventilated, unprovided with privies, and in consequence the streets, which are narrow, unpaved, and worn into deep

ruts, become the common receptacle of mud, refuse, and disgusting ordure ... In Parliament Street (Manchester) there is only one privy for 380 inhabitants, which is placed in a narrow passage whence its effluvia infest the adjacent houses ... [In the factories] well-constituted men are rendered old and past labor at forty ... children are rendered decrepit and deformed and thousands of them slaughtered by consumptions before they arrive at the age of sixteen.[2]

Such accounts can be duplicated almost word for word for New York as late as the 1890's, when half of the city's population lived in old-law tenements, under dreadful conditions.[3] Contemporary descriptions of Calcutta, or observed reality there, are less depressing: life expectancy in Calcutta is certainly higher.

By comparison, life on the farm may seem preferable, even idyllic, as it does now to many Westerners disillusioned with what they see as the deteriorating and soul-destroying quality of life in the modern industrial city. But the nineteenth century West, like the contemporary developing world, was irrevocably committed to economic growth and change. Most young people especially were caught up in its fascination; the ambitious eagerly sought a place in the new world of change and potential upward mobility in the cities, taking their chances that despite the difficult conditions there they could eventually succeed, as most of those did who survived. The security and traditional stability of the village, where change was absent or slow and where only the traditional and by contrast unexciting and unrewarding menial occupations were available, offered to the young only the weakest of counter attractions.

It is the same in the developing world now. High population growth rates (one indication that there has been some real economic improvement) ensure that the rural areas do not in general suffer a net loss of people, but most of the yearly increase is drained away into the cities and there is very little back flow, or "U-turn" migration, despite urban employment problems. Agricultural villages have some capacity to absorb excess labor, especially given the tight-knit and extended family system

characteristic of most of the developing world, but even that capacity has limits. Disappointed returned migrants, or those without the means or courage to migrate in the first place, can be
taken care of by the family, but their labor may often make only
the most marginal contribution to rural production and beyond a
certain point may not justify their keep. Also, once a migrant
leaves, pride requires that he or she make a go of it, or preserve
the illusion of having done so. It is common for migrants to retain
their ties with the village and to return periodically for visits; indeed this is one of the most effective channels for the diffusion of
innovation, or simply of new ideas, from city to countryside. But
their new role as supposed urbanites, adventurers into the outside
world of change, people to whom the stay-at-home villagers expect to look up, makes it difficult for them to return to the village
permanently.

The developing world now is caught in what has aptly been
called "the revolution of rising expectations". Change is in the air;
even those who remain in the villages sense it, and are made specifically aware of the more exciting new world of the city, once
remote and hardly known, through their family and friendship
ties with fellow villagers who have migrated to the cities but who
still regularly visit or correspond with their rural origins. For at
least the first generation, rural migrants to the city commonly return to the village to marry, to bear children, and to attend peri-
odic family events such as funerals; some still own village land. In
many areas of the developing world bus services now link most or
all villages with the cities and with railway lines; there has been
an enormous increase in bus and train travel, and the village
world is no longer isolated. Its perceived "backwardness" stands
out the more sharply, in contrast with what is happening in the
cities. It is understandable that the slow and minimal improvement in village living standards, and the absence of exciting new
alternatives or life styles, should make many want to try their
luck in the cities, where so many of their friends and relatives
have gone.

The revolution of rising expectations feeds on change, and as
the term implies, the ante is continually raised: as change pro-

gresses, people come to expect more and more from it. What small improvements in their circumstances might have left them content a generation, or even five or ten years, ago become no longer sufficient as the pace of change, especially in the cities, quickens and thus continues to draw new migrants from the countryside. Unfortunately, in almost all of the developing world, economic growth, and especially the growth of new jobs, is taking place no faster, or even less rapidly, than population growth. With the additional trends in migration which produce especially high urban population growth rates, it is clear why the cities are so dangerously overcrowded, especially in terms of their ability to absorb the annual increase in those seeking employment. Even for those who do find work, housing and all other basic services are totally inadequate. The revolution of rising expectations merely adds to the bitterness of those millions for whom reality fails miserably to match what they hoped and aimed for, and which others more fortunate have achieved—as is all too clearly displayed in every city. The rewards of "progress" and of more affluent life styles for the few who have succeeded can be seen in films, shops, the beginnings of television, and in newspapers or magazines, all even in small market towns where villagers increasingly travel.

The growing industrial cities present other problems besides overcrowding, unemployment, slums, and frustration. Bad as these are, the more positive or at least more exciting things which are also concentrated in the cities—new careers, new horizons, new technology, new life styles, and new amenities hardly dreamed of by most villagers—continue to feed rising expectations and at the same time rapidly increase the fundamental differences between city and countryside. In the long run, as in the earlier Western-Soviet-Japanese experience, these things, and their fruits in the form of better living standards for all, will theoretically "trickle down" to the countryside and eventually right the balance, at least to some extent. So far, in most of the developing world, this has not taken place nearly as rapidly as urban change, so that the urban-rural gap continues to grow wider. Since in most of the developing world three quarters or more of the population is still rural, and likely to remain so for many years to come, this is hardly a sound development pattern.

Urban over-concentration of economic growth is also in most countries responsible for an overall spatial pattern which is seriously lopsided. The relatively few big cities, most of them on or near the coast (reflecting the origins or recent growth of many of them as colonial outposts of imperialist powers), are tiny dots of development on the outer margins of a vast rural-peasant world which is hardly touched by urban-centered change; peasants see that it is happening, but see also that it affects their material lives as yet very little. Where new urban-generated wealth has come to the countryside, it is too often in exploitative forms, making use of rural labor for urban profit, or further increasing the contrasts between the rural rich and the rural poor.

This has for example been the common result of the so-called "Green Revolution", the spread of higher-yielding varieties of grains developed through research and experimentation in the early 1960's. Only the richer farmers and landowners have been able to afford to grow these new crops, especially since they require much water (usually from irrigation) and commercial fertilizers, which only the better-off can pay for. At least in relative terms, the rural poor have thus grown poorer, in the midst of the new prosperity for a fortunate few—"to them that hath shall be given, and from them that hath shall be taken away, even that which they have." The biblical verse is not wholly inappropriate, since many poorer farmers have indeed been driven out of competition by the Green Revolution and many have lost their land to the newly rich so that they must now work only as hired laborers, or migrate to the cities. Large areas which lack the necessary basis of soil fertility and water supply for the new high-yielding varieties have suffered similarly in the competition. The result of the Green Revolution in its undoubted contribution to total agricultural growth has thus been to distort the benefits of that growth both spatially and socio-economically, leaving the extremes of the urban-rural gap even more widely separated.

But many potential rural resources, including the masses of rural labor (much of it under-employed), are not being fully used by a development pattern so heavily concentrated in a few big cities on the margins of each country. Most industrial production is cheaper when based in large concentrated units, and close to large existing markets which also offer ready capital at lower cost, a pool of already skilled labor, legal, banking, insurance, and shipping services, and an assortment of subsidiary or related industries which are interdependent as sources and users of materials, parts, components, by-products, and technical services. In most of the developing world, transport is inadequate and expensive, especially for the bulk shipments necessary for most industrial operations. What modern transport exists is heavily focused on the big cities, and thus accentuates the pattern of concentration, especially on the coasts where sea transport, by far the cheapest medium, is available. It is difficult and expensive to develop resources or base industrial operations elsewhere. There are sound economic reasons for urban concentration, but the result is both absolute and relative neglect of the potential resources, and the needs, of most people and most areas.

The economic advantages of concentration lead however to still another set of problems, apart from human overcrowding and the miserable conditions under which many city people now live. We have only recently begun to understand a little of the possible consequences of the damage which industrialization does to the physical environment. While the process is not yet as far advanced in the developing as in the "developed" world as a whole, urban concentration there has already produced huge industrial cities—Bombay, Calcutta, Shanghai, Tientsin, Manila, Mexico City, Tehran, and many others—where pollution and environmental degradation are as severe, and as dangerous, as anywhere else. The technology required to eliminate at least the worst of industry-related pollution is now reasonably well known; the only problem is the cost. The Japanese in particular have demonstrated, especially in Tokyo, that industrial and automotive emissions can be kept to low levels and the environment preserved in these terms even in such a highly industrialized and mechanized concentration in the world's largest city. But the cost of such controls is substantial, and of course adds to the cost of the final product, as well as being covered in part from tax revenues or indirectly through government subsidy. This is eminently sound and rational as protection of the quality, perhaps even the viability, of human life in the long run, and is more than worth the financial cost.

One hopes, fervently, that the Japanese example will be followed elsewhere, especially in the United States. But for the much poorer countries of the developing world, it is a terrible dilemma. They urgently need growth, as rapidly and as cheaply as possible, if they are to escape from poverty: given their still rapidly growing populations, they must, like the White Queen in *Alice in Wonderland*, run fast merely in order not to lose ground. Capital funds are scarce and expensive, and are beset by many competing demands, all urgent: for hospitals, for roads, for housing, for steel mills and concrete plants to provide the necessary materials, for chemical fertilizers . . . the list seems to stretch forever. There is neither time nor money to cover all of them adequately, and there won't be for many years to come. These genuinely desperate short-term needs overshadow the longer-term concerns about pollution and environmental degradation, which can be checked for the most part only by incurring increased costs and at the same time slowing down the rate of growth.

The developing countries can in most cases afford neither; they do not have the relative luxury of choice enjoyed by the developed countries. The alternatives, or the costs, are not to be measured in dollars, rupees, or yuan but in the last analysis in human lives, since a delay or an increased cost in the production of steel and cement for hospitals, irrigation projects, housing, transport, or pharmaceutical plants may cost lives which might have been saved by quicker or cheaper growth. The same dilemma applies to the use of pesticides and other chemicals, which can save lives in the urgent present. Countries where insect-borne diseases or crop plant diseases remain a major problem, and where increases in food production still barely exceed population growth rates, are in a totally different position from, for example, the United States in debating whether to ban DDT or Lindane or chemical weed killers. The long-run consequences of environmental degradation are frightening and can cost lives too, possibly even more lives, but the current dilemma of poor countries is obvious.

All this means that cities in the developing world tend to exhibit the worst features of modern industrial urban concentration and have not yet succeeded in improving on the earlier model. They may well be less dreadful than Manchester in 1830 or Pittsburgh in 1880, but those are not the standards by which they are usually judged, especially not by Western observers. As industrialization progresses, they will probably get worse, in all of the above respects, before they get better—better able to provide adequate employment, housing, water, medical and educational services, and a less polluted environment, let alone some amenities of life for most of their inhabitants. And yet they continue to grow. It is not just that the peasants in their rural hinterlands are less critical of them than are outside observers and far more willing to put up with what strikes outsiders as almost unrelieved "squalor". The rural alternatives in the developing world are, after all, very little less "squalid", whatever their other virtues in the eyes of both native and foreign romantic idealists; romantic notions about the beauty, simplicity, and goodness of the village come largely from city people. Villagers go to the cities, however physically unattractive, in pursuit of a wider world of opportunity, as rural people everywhere have always done since cities began. Even if they correctly judge the risks beforehand (which probably very few do), the city draws them, and most of all the biggest cities, where, ironically, both living conditions and prospects for success are worst.

The cities are where the action is; this has been the essence of all cities since the time of Ur and Babylon. There are rewards even for the urban poor, however miserable their housing, in the lights and crowds and spectacles of the city, which may be "squalid" but which is crammed with human action and interaction. Wandering through the crowded, noisy, and colorful bazaars is free, and enjoyable even if one's pockets are empty. There are wedding and funeral processions to watch, parades, open air shows, shops filled with an endless variety of goods, street stalls selling an equal variety, parks, gardens, and monumental public and commercial buildings, houses of the rich and the ordinary, smells of rich, varied cooking, sounds of equally varied vendors, people, and traffic, book stores, sports events, snake charmers and their cultural equivalents, markets and their gossip centers, tea houses, billboard and poster pictures, films, museums—and *people*, of all sorts and conditions and from everywhere. These are the things which make any city exciting no matter what one's own condition. By comparison, the village is Dullsville. Amid all the cosmopolitan bustle of the city there are also usually some people from one's own village or region, for help and emotional security, but also the seemingly endless variety of chances, through wider networks, to move outward and upward into a more sophisticated kind of life. Spend a little time in both villages and cities in the developing world, and it becomes easier to understand what at first seems puzzling: why these already overcrowded and (to an outsider) miserable places continue to grow.

But their continued growth is a dreadful problem, for all the reasons already suggested: worsening of an already lopsided spatial imbalance, neglect of regional resources, galloping pollution, grotesque and dangerous overcrowding, unemployment, slums, frustration and alienation, and further widening of the disastrous economic and ideological gap between city and countryside. Nearly every country in the developing world is concerned about these problems. Many have tried to restrict or to re-direct urban growth so as to ease or minimize the disservice which it seems to create, or even to design wholly new approaches to the city, and to industrialization, which can avoid the problems which development so far has brought, in the same way as it did in the original Western experience which it should now be possible to improve on. Revolutionary China has produced by far the most ambitious effort of this sort, one which has commanded attention all over the world. What are the dimensions and details of this effort, and what are its prospects of success? Can the Chinese succeed where other countries, developed and developing, rich and poor, have so far failed? The answer is important not only for the Chinese fifth of mankind, but perhaps also for the rest of the world, which might be able to learn from a successful Chinese model—as it has learned so much in the past from traditional Chinese civilization.

I have so far avoided the use of the term "Third World", largely because it is ambiguous, and is often used misleadingly, for example, to include everything *outside* North America, Europe, the Soviet Union, Japan, and Australia-New Zealand, as if such a huge and diverse area, three fourths of the world in population, were somehow a coherent region. "Third World" generally means "poor" or "pre-industrial", but the area described above contains numerous countries and regions (e.g., Argentina, Uruguay, Kuwait and other oil-rich states along the Persian Gulf, the Rio and Sao Paulo areas of Brazil, large areas in southern Africa, Singapore, Hong Kong) which are neither poor nor pre-industrial. Europe includes large areas—the Balkans, Sicily, Lapland, much of Greece and Spain—which fit such criteria far more closely. There are clear racial and political overtones to the term "Third World"—"non-European", "non-Western", "victims of exploitation", "backward", and so on. It may be better to avoid them and other ambiguities, by avoiding the term. "Developed" and "developing" are admittedly not much better, but at least they are free of the same sorts of value judgements and do not rest on racial or locational or political criteria, nor on a grab-bag approach, but simply on economics. "Developed" means rich and already industrialized, "developing" the opposite, merely a euphemism for "poor". Obviously, there are degrees of "development", just as there are stages of industrialization, and there are also non-economic and non-industrial measures of "development" which unfortunately do add ambiguity to the use of the term, and which need to be considered now before examining the Chinese experience, and in particular the extent to which China should be included in the general category of "developing" let alone "Third" world.

There is certainly no question about China's relative poverty, or about the still relatively small degree of industrialization there in proportion to the needs of its immense population. China is poor and only beginning to industrialize, as the Chinese themselves repeatedly state. Per capita income figures are notoriously spongy, especially on any international comparative basis, and may often be misleading guides to actual living standards. For China, however, such problems do not arise because we simply do not have the basic data. The Chinese statistical service is very poorly developed, and perhaps for that reason wisely refuses to issue more than a trickle of figures, most of them expressed as percentage increases in production of certain items over preceding years but without stating an original absolute quantitative base so that the percentages cannot be translated into hard numbers. For a discouraging start, we do not even know (nor, apparently, do the Chinese, since high officials have frequently given widely differing figures) what the country's total population is; careful estimates have varied as widely as 100,000,000.[4] We can however accept easily that China is now a poor country, even if it was not so in the past by comparison with the rest of the world.

Poverty and wealth are relative notions, like so many things. As in the revolution of rising expectations, they also vary over time. For at least two thousand years (roughly 200B.C. to 1800A.D.) China was almost certainly richer, *including* the living standards of most of its people, than any other part of the world. It has become poor therefore only recently, absolutely poorer as a combined result of overpopulation and economic stagnation (until the 1950's), but far more relatively poorer, as the commercial and industrial revolutions created vast new wealth in the developed world while China had little part in these changes and fell rapidly behind. But China conforms badly with its supposed peers in the "Third" or "developing" world in most respects except average current living standards and degree of industrialization. Even in economic terms it is unusual, if not unique, as a poor country which nevertheless has no poor people, in the sense that the frightening contrasts between rich and poor so characteristic of the rest of the developing world are absent. Since poverty is relative and there are no rich, poverty in China loses its meaning as well as its bite; certainly living standards are far from luxurious, but at the same time there are virtually no

people living in the kind of material misery so widespread elsewhere in the developing world, especially among the urban poor,
whose conditions seem so much more dreadful for the obvious
contrasts with those of the urban rich who inhabit the same cities.
In that sense, of the bottom of the heap, there are no "poor" people in China. Instead, virtually everyone is poor—at least by
American or European standards.

But there is more to the notion of development than economics. In non-economic terms, China is the reverse of "under-
developed", and is indeed the oldest sophisticated society in the
world. Its two thousand year experience with managing a huge
and complex system of government, production, and human interaction, with brilliant distinction, is unrivalled. These achievements in the past, and what has been accomplished since the
present government came to power in 1949, have rested on the
efforts of a uniquely and coherently organized population coor-
dinating its labor, its managerial talents, and its astonishing capacity for hard work on a set of agreed goals, through a nested
hierarchy of social groups. The Communist state has further re-
fined this impressive instrument for development, used the techniques of group organization and the mass line to inculcate new
revolutionary goals and values, and produced as a result something which perhaps no other society anywhere could hope to
match. China has been able to mobilize its approximately one billion people and to command their united and minutely organized
efforts in the pursuit of planned development. Such a force, as
Mao Tse-tung has said, can indeed move mountains. Can it solve
the problem of the city and devise a better path to industrialization? Like other poor countries, China urgently needs economic
development and is determined to achieve it, or to reach a status
of "developed", in its own terms and timetable, by the end of the
present century, but in its own revolutionary way, which is to be
fundamentally different from the earlier Western-Soviet-Japanese model of urban concentration and its attendant evils.

2. China's Urban and Anti-urban Past

"Men make their own history, but under circumstances
directly encountered, given, and transmitted from the past."

(Marx and Engels, *Selected Works*, 2 vols.,
Moscow: For. Langs. Pub. House, 1970,
Vol. I, p. 225, quoted in M. Meisner,
Mao's China: A History of the P.R.C.,
New York: Free Press, 1977, p. 215.)

CHINA HAS A FOUR THOUSAND YEAR URBAN EXPERIENCE, PROB-
ably longer on a continuous basis than that of any other society.
There have probably been more cities and more urbanites in
China than anywhere else in the world. In that sense, this has
been a sophisticated and highly developed system for a very long
time and constitutes a different background from that of most of
the developing world. The efforts to design new solutions to
urban problems since 1949 are necessarily affected by this long
previous experience and have not been imposed on a *tabula rasa*.
Something like ten per cent of late-traditional China's immense
population lived in cities. Although the level of urbanization remained relatively low, as it was everywhere before the industrial
revolution, the absolute total of urbanites was huge. Cities large
and small are nothing new to China; Sian (*Xian*), Kaifeng,
Hangchow (*Hongzhou*), Nanking (*Nanjing*) and Peking (*Beij-
ing*) have each in its time been the largest cities in the world,
with populations of approximately one million as long as a thousand years ago (Sian and Kaifeng). Especially after the rise of the
imperial system in the third century B.C., Chinese cities were
primarily centers of imperial authority, agents of the bureaucratic

state, and symbolic monuments of the power and majesty of Chinese culture. But although the largest cities owed much of their size to their administrative and managerial functions, they performed commercial and manufacturing functions as well, while many other cities were predominantly centers of trade and industry.

Traditional cities were highly organized, managed, and planned in detail. All of them were walled, in a regular and consistent pattern, with great gates at each of the cardinal points of the compass, from which broad, straight avenues ran to the opposite gate, intersecting in the middle of the city where there was often a drum tower, a plaza, a cluster of official buildings, or a Confucian temple. The major streets, fixing the main axes of the gridiron pattern, divided the city into major quarters which were sometimes also enclosed by their own walls, whose gates were closed at night. Each quarter tended to be functionally specific: warehouses for particular commodities, transport termini, and commercial offices in one sector; retailing in another; manufacturing in another; and others for academies, universities, bookstores, the military establishment and its garrison troops, public food markets, administrative offices, and so on. Most people lived in the same structures which housed their work activities, and within each quarter there were regular lanes organized into neighborhoods, a system often used for the control of urban populations. The emphasis was on order, and on planned management.

The city walls were only secondarily for defense, although they were of course useful in troubled times. Primarily they were symbols of the state-imperial authority, designed to emphasize and glorify the city's role as the seat of power and control, part of an overall imperial plan. The Chinese word for *city* means also *wall*, to distinguish it from smaller market towns without these planned functions. Most cities were founded explicitly by the state, as centers of imperial control and administration responsible for the management (including the defense) of the entire *hsien* (county-size area) which was (and still is) the smallest national administrative unit. The *hsien* city was usually located near the middle of this area, whose size varied inversely with the density of population. One can in fact chart the southward migration of Chinese civilization from its original base on the north China plain by noting the successive establishment of *hsien* cities to control and administer newly-occupied territory, and the multiplication of their number as population increased. From Han times on, these cities, and the provincial capitals, were in effect superimposed, on a naturally varied landscape, in an essentially uniform plan, which makes their imperial origin unmistakable. There was nothing haphazard about Chinese urbanism. China since 1949 has been able to draw on this long accumulation of planning and organizational skills, and on familiarity with many of the problems and challenges posed by cities.

Traditional cities were also centers of both local and long-distance trade, including both inter-provincial and overseas flows. In absolute terms, this trade almost certainly exceeded trade totals in Europe or elsewhere until the nineteenth century. Western observers as late as the 1850's were uniformly impressed by the size and number of Chinese cities and by the hive of organized commercial activity centered in them. Trade was dominated by merchant guilds, highly organized in themselves, but trade and merchants were also taxed and regulated by the bureaucratic state. Some of the major commodities—salt, iron, copper—could be traded in only as part of an official state monopoly, by merchants who were also in effect officials. At many periods, including the most recent centuries, the same was true for foreign trade. But for all merchants except petty local retailers, official approval and official connection were essential to success. Official connections were relatively easy because most merchants (again apart from local small fry) were members of the gentry class, that small minority of the population who had been educated in the classics and passed the imperial examinations (or in a few cases had bought gentry rank). Literacy was in any case essential for their profession, but most gentry families would also have at least one member who was an official—and those engaged in trading in any of the state monopolies were by definition both merchants and officials. Merchants traditionally had lower status, but in practice they prospered as long as they maintained direct or indirect official connections. Much of the manufacturing and mining were also under official control, to produce metals for coinage and weapons or luxury goods for the court and upper classes. Imperial bureaucratic management was imposed even on cities which originally arose primarily as trade or manufacturing centers. The dominant role of the state since 1949 in planning and managing trade, industry, and their urban bases is thus far from new in the Chinese experience.

Unlike cities in the West, especially since the end of the European Middle Ages, traditional Chinese cities were not for the most part agents of change, but rather makers and supporters of the *status quo*. They were after all the seats of imperial power as well as the cosmic centers of the Great Tradition of Chinese civilization. Merchants, who became the chief makers of change and revolution in Western cities, did not constitute a separately powerful group in China who attempted to rival the state or to chart a new course, as in the merchant-dominated cities of early modern Europe such as London or Amsterdam. There was no middle class, in the Western sense, no group such as created the French Revolution in Paris, with a stake in change and an opposite set of interests from the conservative rural areas, where the old land-based hereditary aristocracy and a reactionary royal power were dominant. Western cities represented a different alternative, a different world of change and "progress", which eventually triumphed.

There was no hereditary aristocracy in China, and although merchants managed a very large trade, they owed their success to their cooperation with the state and its system. Merchant-official cooperation was mutually beneficial, and there was no group which stood to improve its position by upsetting the applecart, except for local rebels and those who at long intervals attempted to overthrow the ruling dynasty. Every few centuries such efforts would succeed, but each new dynasty tended to re-establish the traditional system essentially unchanged, reaffirming its successful operation as a means of serving the interests of all parties. The issue was honesty and efficiency, not changing the rules.

Change was of course not absent during the long span of Chinese history, but, especially after about the twelfth century A.D., it was not primarily focused in the cities, which instead were seen as presiding over the "Great Harmony", a persistent Chinese ideal, in which disruptive change was minimized, all groups worked together for the common good, and cities served the countryside as part of a single and symbiotic order. Indeed what pressures there were for change came far more often from the rural areas, as protests against the city-based imperial power or the exploitative accumulation of urban wealth as corruption and self-seeking became more prominent in the last decades of each successive dynasty. The Communist ideal of the city as serving the country as a whole, and as properly supporting rather than challenging the state and its orthodoxy, are thus also well founded in a long Chinese tradition. And part of that tradition includes the role of the countryside as a base for correcting the exploitation or excesses of the city.

The elites in traditional China were city-based (as they are now), but their chief responsibility was the organization, management, defense, and nurturing of the rural base which sustained them, as of course it ultimately sustains all cities everywhere. But the close interdependence of city and countryside was far more explicitly recognized, and indeed welcomed, in China than elsewhere. In the West in particular, when commerce and manufacturing became overwhelmingly dominant as urban functions, the symbiotic tie between city and countryside tended to be obscured or even forgotten. New classes arose in cities—which of course is what the word *bourgeoisie* means; they and the new class of urban proletariat became divorced from the rural context, were indeed different kinds of people with different goals and values. They often scorned rural people as "hicks" or regarded them merely as servants of the city, as providers of food and raw materials, and of cheap labor. These sorts of patterns have tended to spread, with urban-based industrialization, to the rest of the world, including most sharply now its "developing" sectors where the spiritual as well as material gap between city and countryside is a dangerous and worsening problem.

In China there was no such split between urban and rural worlds, and no place in either traditional or contemporary China (despite its avowed Marxism) for Marx's contempt for "the idiocy of rural life". Urban elites may often have exploited the rural sector, but the city's chief function, and its means of existence, was far more clearly seen in China as consisting of the services it provided for the good ordering and productiveness of the countryside which fed it, both literally and metaphorically. It was an agrarian state and an agrarian system. No one questioned that agriculture was the predominant source of wealth (and ultimately of trade goods also), as the land-and-grain tax was the chief source of state revenue. It was agricultural wealth which built the city, and which sustained the power and the cultural magnificence of the empire. Agriculture is still by far the largest sector of the Chinese economy and thus still the basic source of growth potential, including industrial growth. Rural areas hence still support urban efforts at change. State-directed and urban-based efforts were concentrated on enhancing that wealth, including the building and maintenance of water control projects, roads, and waterways, the dissemination of improved techniques, and the protection of the rural areas from disorder. There was a continuous flow of people moving, in both directions, between urban and rural areas, including officials in the course of their duties and rural recruits moving into the commercial or bureaucratic world of the city. Urban-based elites were drawn in the first instance as much from the countryside as from the cities, in keeping with a long tradition, and retained close ties with their rural origins. There was no denigration of rural circumstances and values, but rather, on the part of many urbanites, a longing for the countryside, to which they would retreat whenever they could and to which they almost invariably retired.

The rural sector was recognized as the source of at least as much wisdom and virtue as the city; indeed the literate elite wrote far more admiringly of the countryside than of the "anthill" or the "dusty net" of the city. Most Chinese literature, especially poetry, was written by people who, at least for much of their lives, were also officials; as gentry they had a virtual monopoly of high literacy, and it is hence their picture we have of the Chinese perception of urban and rural worlds. Partly this may reflect the high degree of social mobility characteristic of traditional China, whereby something like a third of the gentry group in each new generation were people from originally humble origins—dominantly rural—who had passed the examinations and acquired gentry rank, which could not be inherited. The openness of this system (until overpopulation began to constrict it after the eighteenth century) no doubt had a lot to do with its long survival, but it also continued to inject rural people and rural values into the urban world.

Traditional Chinese admiration of nature, especially by the poetry-writing elite, is well known, but it was not only beauty that was sought in the nonurban world. Only there, where nature was undisturbed, or where man strove to make it more fruitful as a faithful steward, and was harmoniously attuned to nature's rhythms, was it possible to understand the universe and man's place in it. Rural people were often seen as possessing a better moral character, of simple goodness, while in the cities, where people disregarded nature, truth was clouded and virtue weakened. Only the continual interchange with the countryside kept the city viable. The great sages did not live in cities, nor the happiest people; rural life was regarded not only as pleasanter, but as much closer to the Chinese vision of the good and the true, the only sure path of virtue. As an imperial official in the mid-seventeenth century put it:

> Goodness develops only in the village, evil in the city. The city is the place of commerce and trade. People relate to one another only with the aim of making profits. They are superficial and pretentious. As a result, the city is a sink of iniquities. The village is different. There people are self-reliant and have deep emotional ties with each other.[5]

But how very like Chairman Mao! In this respect too, China since 1949 has been following a long established traditional path, radically different from the Western or modern urban-industrial model, not so much because of Communism as because of Chineseness. For all its revolutionary quality, China remains a very past-conscious society, partly out of understandable pride, partly because of the uniquely long continuous history of a sophisticated tradition. Established patterns of the past may be as important in shaping policy and behavior as more recent revolutionary ideals, but in any case are seldom forgotten or ignored.

China's more recent history, in the century-long confrontation with an imperialist West, has also helped importantly to shape perceptions of the city and of its appropriate nature and role. From the Treaty of Nanking in 1842, which ended the so-called Opium War between China and Britain and gave foreigners special privileges in China, until the end of this treaty system as a consequence of the Second World War and the defeat of Japan, foreigners were free to occupy and control their own trading bases on the coast for the penetration of the China market. Several of these bases grew to become major cities, and by the twentieth century the largest cities in China, as they still are. With the single exception of Peking—and possibly Canton (*Guangzhou*)—all the largest cities of contemporary China owed their major growth to the period when, as "treaty ports", they were under foreign management and benefitted from foreign investment in both trade and manufacturing: Shanghai, Tientsin (*Tianjin*), Wuhan (Hankou), Shenyang (Mukden), Talien (Dairen), Chungking (*Chongqing*), Tsingtao (*Qingdao*), Nanking (see the map on page 32). Altogether, about a hundred Chinese cities were classified as treaty ports, but those listed above were the major ones. Hong Kong remained separate as an outright British colony (as it still is), but played a critical role as an entrepot for the China coast as a whole. Foreigners owned or financed a large share of China's shipping and railways, modern-style banking, and modern-style mining, but within each of the treaty ports foreign control was in practice complete and Chinese authority only nominal. Foreign residents were subject only to the laws of their own countries rather than to Chinese law (extraterritoriality), and their business interests and property were often defended by the use of foreign pressure or even force.

Some of these cities were virtually new (Tsingtao, Talien,

Hong Kong) while others were built beside the walls of an existing Chinese city, as at Shanghai and the other major treaty ports listed above. But all of them represented something new to the Chinese experience, since they were essentially replicas of the modern Western commercial-industrial city, complete with its institutions of banking, insurance, telecommunications, corporate structures with limited liability, joint stock companies, and the protection of impersonal law, Western style, over private property and the accumulation of private wealth. These things, and especially the sanctity of private property and private individual enterprise, had never before been available to Chinese merchants. Many of them were drawn into the rapidly expanding commercial world of the treaty ports. Indeed the population of these cities was from the beginning overwhelmingly Chinese, including laborers to man the new factories and for other manual jobs as well as budding Chinese capitalists, eventually even tycoons, free for the first time from the restrictions of the traditional bureaucratic state and eager to share in the new commercial and industrial wealth. Western industrial technology was prominently displayed in the treaty ports and made them seem like centers of change, progress, and development in a context of Chinese relative technical backwardness and absence of fundamental change. It was in the treaty ports that industrialization began, and it was largely confined there until the 1950's.

But the treaty port experience was on the whole a humiliating one for China. It revealed, as the foreigners were quick to assert, China's "backwardness", and was promoted arrogantly as the model which China must follow.

> The open ports [i.e., treaty ports] are oases of light in a waste of darkness and stagnation . . . All our modern ideas of progress and the possibility of improving their lot seem nonexistent in the official as well as in the popular mind.[6]

> The Chinese city [i.e., at Shanghai] is all inconceivably squalid and offensive to foreign eyes and nostrils, and fills the foreign soul with a sentiment of unutterable disgust. In the foreign settlement all is bustle, enterprise, and progress

... Progress has planted her foot firmly on the banks of the Wusung and from her safe abiding place in the foreign city is sure, slowly but inevitably, to invade and overcome the whole vast empire.[7]

Shanghai became especially notorious for its park along the river, built by the foreigners in Western style to remind them of home, where signs excluded Chinese—and dogs. Chinese merchants profitted from the new business conditions in the treaty ports, but in doing so were to a large extent cut off from their traditional roots and involved in a new world of Western-directed change. Many of them became Westernized, a new kind of Chinese, second or third generation descendants of the compradores (Chinese agents for foreign firms) who had collaborated with the imperialists and aided their invasion of China. This new group of "treaty-port Chinese", as they were called, found the Western example of "progress" and material success compelling, but in the process were increasingly divorced from their own heritage. Political radicals, especially the Communists, called them "running dogs of the foreigners", implying that their collaboration was equivalent to treason. The radicals, and many politically conscious Chinese of all shades of opinion, recognized the treaty ports as an example of success, but largely for foreign profit and at China's expense.

Foreign control in the ports did mean that many dissident Chinese, including outright revolutionaries, fled there for refuge from imperial persecution, and in time the treaty ports became the chief centers of new intellectual ferment. Many Chinese, especially those who lived in the treaty ports and thus were directly exposed to their challenge, were concerned about their country's weakness, its inability to resist foreign pressures, its technological underdevelopment by comparison with Western powers. In the political sanctuary of the treaty ports, but goaded by Western success, they groped for solutions to China's problems. It was there, in Canton and in Shanghai, the largest treaty ports, that the ultimately successful movement was founded for the overthrow of the old imperial dynasty; and there that

modern Chinese nationalism, in the Western sense, was born,
primarily as a reaction to the humiliating blows of foreign imperialism. Imperial China had known no rivals; now for the first time
China was merely one of many countries, in a competition which
left it finishing last, whatever the virtues of its traditional culture.
It was in Shanghai that the Chinese Communist Party was
founded, in 1921, by a group of revolutionaries convinced that
China could never be strong again without radical change, inspired by the example of the Soviet revolution of 1917, but also
determined to resist and eventually expel the foreign model in the
treaty ports and all they stood for as an alien and resented
intrusion.

The treaty ports were thus a continual challenge, a model
which was positive for its demonstration of technological power
but deeply and bitterly negative in its affront to Chinese pride.
The treaty ports never built effective ties with the vast rural hinterland of China, most of which was little affected, except to drain
goods from it for export abroad. They remained isolated foreign
islands on the edge of a far larger Chinese sea. As separate places,
belonging to a separate world and controlled by outsiders, they
were the more easily rejected as alien and their commercial and
industrial success resented as exploitative. In sharp distinction
from traditional Chinese cities with their inward-facing concern
for their rural hinterlands, the treaty ports were outward-facing,
concerned far more with the wider world overseas than with
China. London and New York stock exchange reports and com-
modity prices were more important in Shanghai than news of
what was happening in Szechuan (*Sichuan*) or Hunan. The
treaty ports never functioned as an operative part of the larger
Chinese system as a whole, but many Chinese suffered from foreign arrogance there, in the main bastions of foreign power where
Chinese were often treated as inferior or even "uncivilized" by
Western standards. The bitter nationalist resentment of the
treaty ports is understandable, especially remembering the deep-
seated Chinese pride in their own tradition as a great civilization
which had led the rest of the world for so long.

Bitterness against the treaty ports, which by the 1920's included nearly all China's large cities except for Peking, spilled over into a reaction against the essentially Western kind of city they represented: commercial-industrial concentrations which bred pollution and slums; disruptive change and alienation; large new groups of urban poor and exploited workers; and a much smaller group of new rich, both Chinese and foreign, but with the Chinese apeing Western ways, forsaking Chinese norms and values in favor of the cosmopolitan world of the treaty ports. Nor did the ports serve the country as a whole, cut off as they were from the rural areas which were most of China and its people, and limited to the fringes of the country along the coast where they served only foreign profit. These cities meant alienation and misery, not "progress", or at least not in the form which patriotic Chinese wanted for their country. Early Communist Party figures were especially bitter, for example Tai Chi-t'ao (*Daijitao*):

> Tai's attitude toward Shanghai was the prime catalyst of his commitment to social revolution. For Tai and the entire spectrum of Chinese revolutionaries, she was a bitch-goddess who gnawed at their souls, scarring them brutally and indelibly. Life in the Concessions (foreign-controlled areas) was comparatively safe, but the very security which Tai enjoyed there galled and tormented him at the same time. He, a Chinese, was being protected from fellow Chinese by the grace and scientific superiority of Westerners. His asylum rapidly crystallized into a personal confrontation with the entire legacy of China's humiliations at the hands of the West.[8]

The Communist perception of the treaty ports, and of the foreign kind of city they represented, was however cemented even more directly and firmly by their own experience in their effort to win political power through revolution. In the 1920's they tried again and again to follow the Soviet example (as they were also urged to do by Soviet advisers in China) by organizing the urban proletariat and with their help seizing power first in the cities. Attempted uprisings in Changsha (*Qangxa*), in Canton, and in

Shanghai ended in complete failure, and nearly wiped out the Party. The problem was not merely that the urban proletariat was still small, much smaller even proportionately than in Russian cities, but these supposed potential revolutionaries, according to the Marxist formula, were not willing to join the struggle, apparently corrupted beyond redemption by the bourgeois atmosphere of the treaty ports, or with their supposed revolutionary vision blurred by that contamination. The treaty ports were also the strongholds of the rival political party, the Kuomintang (*Guomindang*), which had built its power on a coalition of landlords, compradores, and treaty port business men, with the latter dominant. The Kuomintang police and army, which controlled the Chinese majority in the treaty ports, relatively easily crushed the Communists' successive efforts at urban revolution and left them only a tiny remnant, obliged to flee for survival to the remote rural areas.

That experience increased Communist bitterness against the cities (treaty ports) and left them with an anti-urban legacy which still persists. Defeated and almost annihilated in the cities, the Communists retreated to countryside, where under Mao's leadership they succeeded in building a political base among the peasants, who had not been exposed to the corrupting bourgeois influences of the cities. Here was the *real* China, largely untouched by the alien influences of the treaty ports and true to the Chinese tradition. It was only there that a genuinely *Chinese* answer to Western pressures, and a Chinese solution to the country's problems, could be generated.

> To rely on the peasants, build rural base areas, and use the countryside to encircle and finally capture the cities—such was the way to victory in the Chinese revolution. Comrade Mao Tse-tung pointed out the importance of building revolutionary base areas: "Since China's key cities have long been occupied by the powerful imperialists and their reactionary Chinese allies, it is imperative for the revolutionary ranks to turn the backward villages into advanced consolidated base areas, into great military, political, economic and

cultural bastions of the revolution from which to fight their vicious enemies who are using the cities for attacks on the rural districts, and in this way gradually to achieve the complete victory of the revolution through protracted fighting." The imperialists usually begin by seizing the big cities and the main lines of communication, but they are unable to bring the vast countryside completely under their control . . . The countryside and the countryside alone can provide the revolutionary bases from which the revolutionaries can go forward to final victory . . . The contemporary world revolution also presents a picture of the encirclement of the cities by the rural areas.[9]

This formula for the road to political power proved successful, and the peasant armies of the Communists marched into Shanghai and the other treaty ports in 1949, to reclaim them for China, but also to re-make them, change their nature, and build a new China in which cities would play a more constructive and genuinely national role. Their bourgeois poison and foreign cosmopolitan character must be eradicated, their growth restricted, and their industrial capacity turned to serve the rural areas and to help build new industrial bases in the previously neglected hinterland, where the great majority of Chinese lived. One of the Communist criticisms of the treaty ports was also that they had virtually monopolized what modern manufacturing had developed in China (much of it under foreign control) and yet were limited to a few spots along the outer edge of the country and the navigable Yangtze River (see the map on page 32) where they could more easily drain China's wealth abroad. The treaty ports contained over 90 per cent of China's pre-1949 industrial plant, a heavily lopsided pattern within any national context. Over a third of China's "modern" industrial investment, labor force, and output were in Shanghai alone; nearly all the rest was in the Liao River valley of south-central Manchuria, the Tientsin area, the Wuhan (Hankou) area on the Yangtze, and a few other major treaty ports also accessible to ocean shipping. Such over-concentration was undesirable in itself, and was also strategically un-

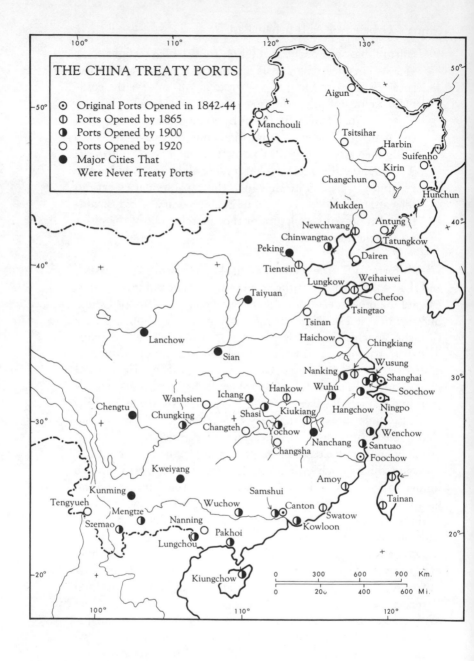

THE CHINA TREATY PORTS

- ⊙ Original Ports Opened in 1842-44
- ◐ Ports Opened by 1865
- ◑ Ports Opened by 1900
- ○ Ports Opened by 1920
- ● Major Cities That Were Never Treaty Ports

Aigun

Manchouli

Tsitsihar

Harbin

Suifenho

Kirin

Changchun

Hunchun

Mukden

Antung

Newchwang

Tatungkow

Chinwangtao

Peking

Dairen

Tientsin

Lungkow

Weihaiwei

Taiyuan

Chefoo

Tsingtao

Tsinan

Lanchow

Haichow

Sian

Chingkiang

Wusung

Nanking

Shanghai

Hankow

Wuhu

Soochow

Wanhsien

Ichang

Hangchow

Ningpo

Chengtu

Shasi

Kiukiang

Chungking

Changteh

Yochow

Wenchow

Changsha

Nanchang

Santuao

Kweiyang

Foochow

Kunming

Amoy

Tengyueh

Samshui

Tainan

Mengtze

Wuchow

Canton

Szemao

Nanning

Swatow

Lungchow

Pakhoi

Kowloon

Kiungchow

| 0 | 300 | 600 | 900 | Km. |
| 0 | 200 | 400 | 600 | Mi. |

sound, exposing the country's most vulnerable and vital sector to maximum risk from the maritime imperialist powers, including Japan, so recently China's destructive enemies and now, especially with the Korean war (1950–53), doubly hostile to the new Communist government.

But the chief need was seen as changing these cities inherited from colonialism to serve the nation as a whole instead of their former foreign owners, and to change their character accordingly. At the same time, new cities, of the approved sort, must be built in the rest of the country as necessary bases for the now urgently needed economic and technological development of China, most of which had been touched hardly at all by development in the treaty ports. It was a tall order, and one for which the Communists, fresh from their long struggle in the rural areas and suspicious of all cities, from which they had been isolated in any case for twenty years, were poorly prepared. But the revolutionary challenge was clear, and time was pressing:

> So many deeds cry out to be done,
> And always urgently.
> The world rolls on,
> Time passes.
> Ten thousand years are too long;
> Seize the day, seize the hour,
> Our force is irresistible.[10]

3. Controlling and Dispersing Urban Growth

COMMUNIST CHINA'S OVERRIDING DEVELOPMENT GOAL IS IN-dustrialization. China has "stood up" as a nation and regained its pride, but it must now regain its strength, which must come from making up for the years while its economy and its technological level stagnated as the West and Japan forged ahead. The Chinese leaders acknowledge that their country is poor; and although there has been rapid industrial growth it is still small relative to the huge population, and still less sophisticated or efficient than in the developed economies. It is also clear that although agricultural production has continued to increase, population has increased almost as rapidly and there has probably been only a slight rise in average living standards, as far as these can be estimated given the inadequacy of data. The margin remains precarious and the need for rapid growth is urgent. It is also a matter of pride for the Chinese, the strong national pride which has for so long been part of the Chinese character, but also the pride of a new revolutionary state which believes, or asserts, that it has designed a better model for development than earlier Western models, and must now deliver the goods.

The ideological side of the revolution may however be as important as its drive for economic development, and the two are potentially in conflict on many points. The chief focus of this potential conflict is the city, where industrialization is still largely based, and where the urban problems familiar in the rest of the world are also evident. The Maoist blueprint for a better world may be reduced, as Mao himself has done, to two goals: eliminate the distinctions between mental and manual labor, and eliminate the differences between city and countryside. The two are of course interrelated, since mental labor, and the elites who engage in it, are almost entirely urban. In keeping with traditional Chinese attitudes, but further reinforced by the Communist Party's struggle for power, originally *against* the cities, the Maoist attitude toward cities and the elites they breed is negative. Honesty, virtue, hard work, and plain living are to be found primarily among the peasants; it was their revolutionary vision which won the struggle, and which can now create a new China. Their vision is pure, untainted by city living, and as 80 per cent of the population they constitute a vast reservoir of revolutionary potential. The rest of the population—the urban sector—must learn from the peasants, re-make their lives and their minds on that model. At the same time, the rural areas must be transformed by the new technology emanating from the cities. In this process, the cities will help to raise the economic level of the rural areas while restricting their own, and the differences between the two will in time disappear.

The Great Leap Forward in 1957 was an attempt, directed by Mao, to achieve such a result through mass mobilization of peasant drives to create industrialization by their own local efforts, as in the famous "backyard steel furnaces", while at the same time also increasing agricultural production. It ended in a considerable degree of chaos, and for a few years such radical efforts were abandoned and the economy allowed to recover. The Cultural Revolution of 1966–68 was another such radical effort, aimed specifically at cutting down urban elites and Party cadres, who were accused of forgetting their duty to "serve the people", neglecting rural development and promoting instead "revisionist" and bourgeois (i.e., urban) values. The pendulum swung back more slowly after the Cultural Revolution, but with the death of Mao in 1976, and especially after the renewed rise to power of Teng Hsiao-p'ing (*Dengxiaoping*) from 1978, the balance appears to have shifted away from the visionary radical line and in favor of a more apolitical emphasis on economic growth *per se*. As Teng himself remarked some years earlier during the political controversy over the Cultural Revolution, "I don't care if a cat is white or black, so long as it catches mice". Such a point of view implies, as Teng clearly meant it to do, that ideological visions should be sacrificed for the rapid development which China so badly needs, and which can take place fastest in cities, with professional elites and "experts", drawing on foreign expertise and technology, rather than relying on peasants or on rural areas and their alternative and self-reliant efforts at development. But Mao's vision remains compelling for a still revolutionary China:

> China's six hundred million people have two remarkable peculiarities; they are first of all poor, and secondly blank. That may seem like a bad thing, but it is really a good thing. Poor people want change, want to do things, want revolution. A clean sheet of paper has no blotches, and so the newest and most beautiful words can be written on it, the newest and most beautiful pictures can be painted on it.[11]

That sets an exciting challenge, still attractive to many Chinese, and to others elsewhere who have been caught by the fascination of the Maoist vision, including those who see the modern industrial city as one of the world's most serious problems and who seek a better solution. China does indeed have great potential for revolutionary change. It also has the opportunity, before the clean sheet of paper has been more than marginally blotched by Western-style urban-industrial concentration, to devise a better way. The conflict between revolutionary vision and urgent cost-economics will continue for a long time in China, however the balance between them may shift from time to time. There is still a basic commitment to organized group effort, an old Chinese tradition long before Communism gave it added meaning as "the mass line". There is still a greater willingness than in other societies to submit individual interest to group interest, again as there traditionally was but which has become even more firmly established since 1949. A traditional Chinese proverb, often cited by the Communists, puts this as a matter of common interest: "When there is water in the big river, the little streams will be full also". It is both a Chinese and a Communist trait to build on this acceptance of the paramountcy of the group, and the nation, as the best way to ensure both individual and mass welfare. But such a pattern can also be a highly effective strategy for economic development, as indeed China has already demonstrated. Within that context, China's efforts to develop, and in particular to reshape the nature and function of cities, seem certain to remain distinctive. What in fact has been accomplished since 1949?

In the first flush of the revolution's victory, and with the bitter memory of the treaty ports still fresh, there was talk of actually dismantling the major east-coast cities, Shanghai in particular, and relocating their industrial plant in better distributed inland centers. It was soon realized that however attractive such a move might be ideologically or emotionally, it made little sense in practical terms. Industrialization in the rest of the country was dependent on what only Shanghai and the other former treaty ports could produce; to disrupt the existing bases would be to cripple the drive for development. China was also now, by its own choice (further underlined by a United Nations blockade and embargo resulting from the Korean War) on its own, "self-reliant", and could not depend on imported technology, materials, or experts. After the split with the Soviet Union and the withdrawal of Soviet aid in 1958–59, China was truly alone. Development of the rest of the country could come only from existing Chinese industrial capacity and skills, and these were almost entirely in the former treaty ports.

It was common to complain that this lopsided concentration along the coastal fringe resulted from imperialist motives to maximize the drainage overseas of China's wealth for their own profit and to the disregard of the needs of the rest of the country. Certainly the foreign owners and investors sought to maximize their profits and were not particularly concerned with Chinese national development goals. But the sites of the major treaty ports and their industrial and commercial establishments were chosen with a close eye to costs—or rather those cities which grew largest did so because of clear economic advantages, essentially unrelated to politics, planning, or ideology. The major treaty ports were and still are the points of least cost for both manufacturing and trade bases, primarily as a result of transport. They remain the chief foci of rail, water, and road networks (including coastal sea transport, the cheapest of all); they can assemble raw materials and distribute finished goods more cheaply than any alternative sites. Partly as a result, but also because they became the biggest cities and industrial centers, they also offered the lowest cost electric power and other energy sources, and in largest volume. In addition, they had by far the largest pool of skilled labor, technicians, and managers; by far the best source of capital at lowest cost; and by far the best spread of other services: banking, insurance, shipping, and ancillary or related enterprises as users or sources of materials, by-products, components, and technical services. And although these cities were so heavily concentrated in the coastal fringe, on the extreme edge of the country, they are still closely related to the center of the China market, since the bulk of China's population is in the east (see the map on page 39).

The spatial distribution of manufacturing, or of "development" more generally, in the United States (as in nearly all countries) is really not that different, as illustrated in the map on page 41. Spatial concentration is a basic part of the nature of modern economic development, in every part of the world, and especially of industrialization, the engine of all other development. A few areas and a few sites have overwhelming advantages for industrialization; it makes sense to concentrate growth there. The problem then becomes one of how to distribute the benefits of development to the rest of the country. This is never done perfectly anywhere; there will always be regional differences and disparities, and in particular a gap between city and countryside. But the distribution process obviously takes place most effectively in areas where mobility is high: where transport is abundant and relatively cheap so that goods, services, and people can

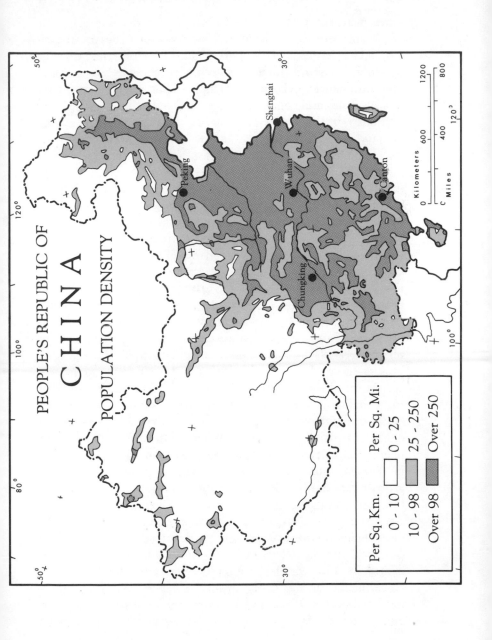

PEOPLE'S REPUBLIC OF
CHINA
POPULATION DENSITY

Per Sq. Km.		Per Sq. Mi.
0 - 10		0 - 25
10 - 98		25 - 250
Over 98		Over 250

Peking

Shanghai

Wuhan

Chungking

Canton

Kilometers
0   200   400   600   800   1000   1200
Miles

move more easily. The United States is a good example; most goods and services available in New York or Chicago are also available in Alabama or Montana, and it is also relatively easy for individuals to move around in search of special goods or services, or to shift base entirely and seek employment in what they regard as a more desirable place.

China is at the other end of the mobility spectrum, as a huge country (larger than the U.S. in area and with nearly five times its population) with a distribution system (transport, telecommunications, labor mobility) still very little developed, totally inadequate to the scale of the country, and hence both chronically overburdened and very expensive. Industrial-urban concentration in China is understandable in these terms, as is the weakness of the distribution system in attempting to narrow the urban-rural gap. As transport and mobility improve and costs come down, however, urban concentration will not disappear but if anything will increase, as it has elsewhere, unless specific, and probably uneconomic, measures are taken to prevent this. Alternatively, steps can be taken to ensure that the new benefits of urban-based industrialization are distributed better to rural and remote areas. China since 1949 has in effect tried to do both. A peasant-centered revolution, coming to power from rural bases against the cities, and ruling a country which is still 80 per cent rural and agricultural, could hardly do otherwise.

But there is nevertheless a hard choice to be made between revolutionary goals for national-rural development for all on the one hand, and rapid economic-industrial growth on the other. At least in the short run, the two are in conflict. Economic-industrial growth can clearly take place most rapidly and most cheaply through continued urban concentration. Later on it may be possible to improve distribution, but the need for rapid and cheap development in this poor and marginal but proud and ambitious country is urgent, and urgently felt. And yet the pull of the original revolutionary vision also remains strong; its emotional hold is powerful, but it also speaks from the reality of a dominantly rural and peasant China and addresses its problems directly. Industrialization took place in the West essentially without plan,

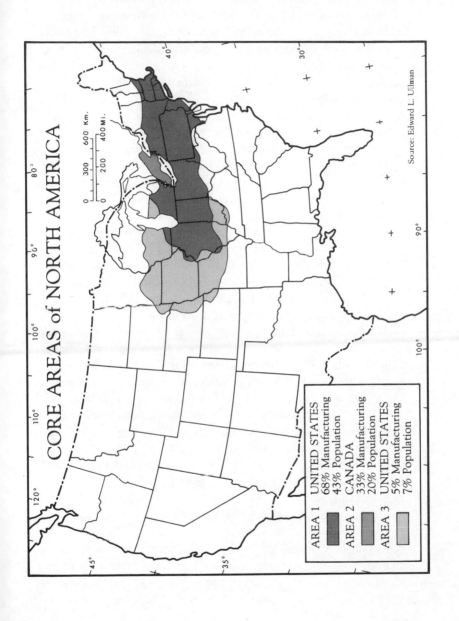

CORE AREAS of NORTH AMERICA

AREA 1 UNITED STATES
68% Manufacturing
43% Population

AREA 2 CANADA
33% Manufacturing
20% Population

AREA 3 UNITED STATES
5% Manufacturing
7% Population

0 300 600 Km.
0 200 400 Mi.

Source: Edward L. Ullman

following the patterns of economic advantage and the pressures of the marketplace. China is inspired by its revolution, by its traditional legacy, by its experience with the treaty ports, and by its critical analysis of Western bourgeois capitalism, to *plan* a better path. Whatever one's political persuasion, one can only wish the planners well. And it is understandable that many in the West cherish the hope that somehow the Chinese can produce a form of development which avoids the worst mistakes of the Western model and leads the way to a better world for all of us, as the Maoist vision indeed promises.

The city is the major focus of this issue, as it has been of all development everywhere so far. What has been happening with the Chinese city? In brief, the cities have been notable as problem areas and as thriving development centers, both it would seem in about equal amounts. There is deep concern about overcrowding, over-concentration, and "bourgeois values", but also pride in new industrial achievements. There does not seem as yet to be any clear resolution of the conflict between urban-centered growth on economic grounds and rural-centered growth on ideological-revolutionary grounds. Both are being pursued simultaneously, as is perhaps only to be expected. The Maoist revolutionary goals are simply too important, too prominent, too appealing, too distinctly Chinese—and even too commonsensical—to ignore, while the strictly economic development goals are too urgent in a practical sense. The question is one of the balance between the two, a balance which has fluctuated widely between the extremes of the Great Leap and Cultural Revolution and the supposedly "revisionist" policies of Liu Shao-ch'i (*Liuxiaoqi*) and Teng Hsiao-p'ing. But it was the *problems* of the big cities which first spurred the new revolutionary government into action.

It seems reasonably clear that the Communist victory came faster than anyone expected, and that the new government in 1949 was far from ready to manage the huge set of problems involved in administering, let alone planning for, this immense country suffering from the devastating effects of more than fifteen years of war, which had begun in 1931 with the Japanese invasion of Manchuria, escalated in 1937 with their attack on

Shanghai, and continued as civil war after Japan's defeat until 1949. With the restoration of order and the re-establishment of the major transport routes, people understandably flocked to the cities, where there was at least the possibility of a better life than in the war-torn and backward countryside. The population of all of the big cities boomed. Perhaps as many as 20 million people migrated from rural to urban areas between 1949 and 1957, although the precise number must remain unclear in part because many were illegal migrants who tried to avoid controls, and hence were not recorded.[12] The problem was recognized quickly and efforts made to return many people to their rural homes, but with substantial economic recovery after 1950 the rural-urban gap in living standards began to widen rapidly and rural migrants again flooded into the cities.

The rapid increase in urban populations was well beyond the cities' ability to house, feed, or provide jobs for them—the familiar problem in all cities in the developing world. Many migrants lived in squatter camps, unfortunately for them too conspicuous to avoid counter measures. But though such camps were frequently cleaned out and their occupants sent back to their villages, the back flow seems to have been almost equally heavy; the difference was that the government published figures for those it had sent back from urban to rural areas, but less often (and far less complete) for those who managed to return to the city in defiance of regulations, whose success of course depended on their escaping official notice. In Shanghai alone, the municipal administration estimated that by the end of 1956 at least 60,000 people were living in the city illegally (i.e., without registration cards or ration coupons which by then were required of everyone), which pretty clearly was a good deal less than the real total even for this one city. Also, deportation was applied, apparently, only to migrants who had not found urban jobs and hence had no one to speak for them. A large share of the migrants presumably therefore were allowed to remain, as against the figures for those who were deported, although the precise numbers must remain a guess.[13] Meanwhile, urban birth rates apparently (we have no reliable statistics) remained high, and with the added pressure from migrants who were predominantly in the younger, higher-fertility age group, the cities became dangerously overcrowded.

In the chaos of the Great Leap of 1957–58 and its aftermath there were apparently new large scale rural-urban population movements as peasants fled the disorganized countryside for the cities. Some sources suggest that this flow again reached 20 million in both 1958 and 1959.[14] But with the failure of the Leap and the return to more conservative and centralized planning, massive efforts were made to restrict urban growth and even to roll back city population totals to what was felt to be manageable levels. Earlier controls, imposed beginning in 1953, were made increasingly stringent. Urban employers were forbidden to hire or recruit rural migrants; no one was legally permitted to remain in the city without a work permit, an approved place in a registered household, and a food ration card; travel was by permit only (all of these regulations are still in force, although travel has recently become a little easier). Migrants who did not fulfill these conditions were stopped and turned back in transit at checkpoints in railway stations and other transport junctions. In addition, very large numbers of people—one estimate suggests 20 million in the one year of 1961—were "reassigned" from cities and returned to the countryside, in an effort to produce a reduction in total urban population, especially in the biggest cities.[15] The official policy was stated in 1963 by Po I-po, Chairman of the State Economic Commission, as follows:

> We have drawn too much manpower from the rural areas to the cities. Natural calamities show that our urban population is greater than what our countryside can supply. While our industry has been modernized, our agriculture has not yet been mechanized. And until the mechanization of agriculture, our urban population must be reduced from 130 million to 110 million.[16]

This was clearly in response, among other things, to the agricultural problems which followed the collapse of the Great Leap, when for several years between 1959 and 1963 there were severe food shortages which were especially troublesome in the big cities. The failure of the Great Leap was a sharp reminder that China's development had still a long way to go, and that its pace was far from fast enough to absorb new recruits to the labor force in the urban industrial sector, let alone to feed and house them. Total urban employment may have increased by about three million jobs from 1953 to 1957, but the total urban labor force seeking work grew by about one million each year, thus leaving about a quarter of them without jobs.[17] This is about the same scale of unemployment as in Indian cities, where reasonably accurate statistics are available, and probably in most cities in the developing world. The difference in China is the unparalleled power of the central state, at least to attempt imposed solutions by forcibly preventing migration to the cities and by re-assigning redundant urbanites to rural areas.

At the same time, there was an almost regretful acknowledgement that the cities, and especially the biggest of them, were the essential heart of China's development drive and that it therefore made little sense to handicap them. The early years following 1949 were a time of euphoria and of high expectations, of revolutionary visions of a genuinely new China in which cities would be cut down to size, transformed in nature, and re-shaped to serve a countryside which would become the center of the development stage. But the first five-year plan begun in 1953 produced a rate of growth which the leaders rightly found unsatisfactory in all respects: agricultural and industrial production were both rising far too slowly. At a meeting of the Political Bureau of the Central Committee of the Party in April of 1956 which reviewed economic progress to date, it was concluded that the rate of industrial growth must be increased; and it was recognized that agricultural output, still rising only about as fast as population, could be rescued from this critical position only by new inputs—fertilizers, irrigation equipment, for instance—from the industrial sector. It was perhaps the first major acknowledgement that China's development problem was immense, as intractable as that for any other poor country but far more monumental if only because of China'a size, and that revolutionary enthusiasm alone was not a sufficient answer.

The industrial sector was of course in the cities, and especially in the largest cities. At the 1956 meeting Chairman Mao issued a major document, *On the Ten Great Relationships*, which identified the ten most urgent problems stemming from planning decisions taken since 1949. The most important of these dealt with the location of industry and the role of existing large cities:

> In the past few years we have not laid enough stress on industry in the coastal regions. I think we should make some changes ... The technical level of coastal industry is high, the quality of its products good, its costs low, and it produces many new products. Development of coastal industry will have a stimulating effect on the technical level and quality of national industry as a whole ... If we do not use the industry of the coastal region, we cannot establish industry in the interior. We must not simply maintain coastal industry. We must also develop it where appropriate.[18]

This put the problem pointedly and accurately—but it came nevertheless from the arch-ideologue, the revolutionary Helmsman! The coastal cities were so prominent and essential not as the result of an imperialist plot but because they made practical, economic sense. However politics or foreign privilege or bourgeois investment may have affected this pattern in the past, the fact remained that it was in the coastal cities that China's potential for development lay, including its hopes for building industry in the rest of the country. That would take steel and machines, technicians and workers, which could come only from the existing coastal centers.

The Chinese development strategy was roughly modelled on the Soviet experience, in emphasizing the development of new inland cities, but these had to be provided with both funds and equipment from the existing coastal bases. During the first five-year plan period, for example, Shanghai provided about 18 per cent of the central government's revenue budget but received only about 2 per cent of central investment funds in return, as Shanghai in effect subsidized the building of new inland industrial cities.[19] Skilled workers and machinery, somtimes whole plants, were transferred from Shanghai to places like Lanchow (*Lanzhou*) in Kansu (*Gansu*) and to distant Sinkiang (*Xinzhiang*) where the provincial capital at Urumchi was transformed into an industrial center. During the 1950's about one fifth of the gross value of industrial output in China came from Shanghai alone, although in the critical category of machinery Shanghai's share was much larger.[20] After Mao's statement at the 1956 meeting, there appears to have been an increase in new industrial investment in Shanghai and other coastal cities, as the statement urged, but it almost certainly has remained considerably less than these cities' contribution to GNP. The critical measure has been to avoid milking the coastal cities to the point where their ability to continue producing is impaired, something which the planners appear to have understood clearly. At the same time, it is reasonable enough in the light of any effort at *national* development that these cities should contribute to a better spatial pattern of growth and to the rise of new industrial centers in the rest of the country. There has also been a continuing trend toward using the more sophisticated industrial plant in the coastal cities to turn out high quality finished goods from semi-finished or lower-quality components produced by smaller plants in inland centers where the technical level is lower: the final processing of metals, for example, or the assembly and precision-control finishing of machines and machine-building equipment.[21]

But the problem of housing, feeding, and employing urban residents remains, and controls are still imposed since, left to themselves, people would continue to move from the poorer countryside to the more developed cities, as everywhere else in the developing world and for exactly the same reasons. These have often been described as a mixture of "push" and "pull" factors: limited economic opportunity or actual suffering in rural areas pushes migrants out, and wider opportunity, variety, stimulation, and the prospect of higher incomes and status pulls them to the cities. China has succeeded, apparently, no better than other developing countries in correcting this imbalance by creating enough new economic opportunity and other advantages in rural areas to make them more attractive, or by producing rapid enough growth of urban employment and basic services such as housing to absorb the millions of would-be migrants. What the Chinese alone have apparently been able to do is arbitrarily to control the growth of at least the largest cities. This uniquely powerful government can nevertheless not create economic growth merely by state power, or at least not significantly faster than other governments elsewhere in the developing world. The revolution has produced no magic formula, despite mass move- ments such as the Great Leap, to catapult China out of poverty. Economic development anywhere is hard and slow, and there are no short cuts. What the Chinese government can do, as no other government has succeeded in doing, is to limit the movement of its people. That is no mean accomplishment, even if it begs the fundamental question.

Chinese population statistics are so poor, fragmentary, and often self-contradictory, that one can derive no precise picture of the dimensions of this accomplishment, even for the single largest city of Shanghai. There is an unacceptably wide range of figures, from supposedly "official" sources, purporting to give the popu- lation of Shanghai. One cause of ambiguity is that the municipal administrative area of the city is in fact about 80 per cent rural- agricultural, an area of intensive cultivation designed to feed the city and hence densely populated, but hardly "urban". Most pop- ulation totals for Shanghai include this very large area as if it were part of the city, which it is only administratively. The same administrative arrangement obtains at Tientsin and Peking, the other two of the three biggest Chinese cities, each administered separately from the provinces where they are located. This move was made following the Great Leap and the ensuing food crises primarily in order to insure that each big city, through its control over its immediate rural hinterland, would be responsible for most if not all of its own food supply.

Shanghai is often referred to in the foreign press as the world's biggest city (although with widely different totals) because most sources lump the population of the large rural area in with the genuinely urban population. Once this has been sorted out, and based on fragmentary reports in the Chinese press, it seems reasonably clear that *urban* Shanghai grew out of control in the 1950's as a result of inadequately restricted rural in-migration and may have reached 6 ½ million, but that following the imposition of strict controls and the reassignment of large numbers every year to the countryside the urban total was reduced to about 5 ½ million (plus about 5 million in the rural parts of the Shanghai Municipality) and successfully held at roughly that figure until sometime in the 1970's. Approximately the same order of success seems to have been achieved with the other big cities (with the possible exception of Peking, whose expanded administrative as well as new industrial functions produced massive population growth). What urban population growth has taken place since is presumably still kept in some sort of balance with increased jobs as development proceeds, and with increased supplies of food, housing, and other basic urban services.[22] By the 1970's China's determined if belated efforts to control overall population growth—pressure for late marriage, widespread availability of, and propaganda for, contraception and abortion, pressure to conform to the national norm of small families, and use of housing and work assignments and ration allotments as both positive and negative sanctions—had probably also begun to depress the birth rate, and especially in the cities where all these efforts at control could be most effective.[23]

One part of the job of re-making the urban scene in China has thus been at least well begun: limiting the further growth of the biggest cities, and using their industrial strength to fuel new urban-industrial development in the rest of the country in a spatially more balanced pattern. The map on page 50 shows the degree of dispersal already achieved. The coastal cities—former treaty ports—are still the largest single industrial bases, but their share of the national total continues to fall as new bases grow inland: at least one major industrial center in each of China's provinces. There have been consistent efforts, through successive adjustments in economic regionalization schemes, to make each major economic region as self-sufficient industrially as possible, partly to lessen the heavy strain on the transport system, partly to spur the use of previously neglected regional resources, and

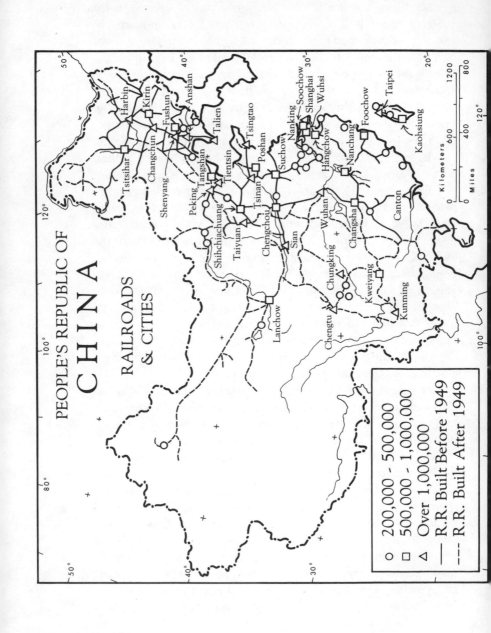

PEOPLE'S REPUBLIC OF
CHINA
RAILROADS
& CITIES

○ 200,000 - 500,000
□ 500,000 - 1,000,000
△ Over 1,000,000
— R.R. Built Before 1949
- - - R.R. Built After 1949

Harbin
Kirin
Tsitsihar
Changchun
Fushun
Anshan
Shenyang
Talien
Peking
Tangshan
Tientsin
Tsingtao
Poshan
Tsinan
Shihchiachuang
Taiyuan
Chengchou
Suchow
Nanking
Soochow
Shanghai
Wuhsi
Hangchow
Nanchang
Foochow
Taipei
Kaohsiung
Sian
Wuhan
Changsha
Canton
Chungking
Kweiyang
Kunming
Lanchow
Chengtu

Kilometers
0   400   800   1200
Miles
0   400   600

50°   40°   30°   20°
120°
100°
80°
100°
120°

partly to stimulate regional development for its own sake, to make up for the previously lopsided pattern of treaty port days. But it is recognized that for many things, especially more sophisticated machines and technology, the former treaty ports are the most efficient or the only source; their development must be enhanced despite the original revolutionary bias against them, as the necessary price for national development in any form. The revolutionary vision of a peasant-rural China in command, which would drive the cities from the center of the development stage—and especially the former treaty ports—has had to be compromised as the hard facts of the struggle for development revealed the vital role which urban industrial concentrations must play, even in a new revolutionary China.

The city still occupies the leading role in China's development. And while industrial dispersal and the building of new urban bases inland makes obvious sense for national development goals, it is still an urban-centered growth concentrated in cities. We lack adequate data, but although there seems to have been substantial dispersal and growth of new inland cities in the 1950's, there has been little change since about 1958 in the relative share of regions of the country in the gross value of industrial output, and approximately the same industrial growth rate for coastal and inland regions. If one omits oil (which is primarily just extraction rather than manufacturing) as an industrial category, inland areas have grown much less industrially than the old coastal areas since 1957.[24] New or expanded cities in inland provinces are freer of the treaty port taint, but they are cities nevertheless, many of them over a million in population, and still more over half a million. While it is official policy to prevent urban "giantism" and to keep these newer cities substantially smaller than the huge coastal conurbations, it is much more difficult to prevent their acquiring the kinds of characteristics which have made the Chinese consistently distrust cities: elitism, "expertism", bourgeois attitudes and life styles, and growing alienation from the vast rural-peasant majority. The root meaning of "bourgeois"—a city dweller—is no accident, and acquires a specially pointed significance in the context of the Chinese experience, both traditional and modern.

It is understandable that revolutionary planners should still be tempted to somehow reduce if not wholly to eliminate dependence on city growth as the path to the development which China so badly needs; to chart a brave new course for this peasant country and to avoid the over-concentration, pollution, alienation, and elitism which urban-based industrial growth seems inevitably to bring. What would be lost by such a policy? Unfortunately, the Chinese have progressively recognized that the answer tends to be "everything", since everything depends on industrialization and since that can be produced fastest and cheapest in urban concentrations. The achievement of other, non-economic revolutionary goals, although equally important, would be hollow and meaningless if they were won in a context of continued poverty. Mass welfare has rightly been given top priority; and the price which that decision exacts includes the continued growth of cities. Chapter 5 examines what has been happening in these cities, as the state has tried to re-shape them away from their bourgeois origins or tendencies and to plan for their more appropriate socialist development. Meanwhile, the following chapter deals with the rural sector, and the peasant-based alternative to urban concentration as a development strategy. To what extent and in what ways has the original revolutionary vision been realized there, even if it has had to compromise its position on the city itself?

4. Walking on Two Legs

THE MAOIST VISION STILL HOLDS A PROMISE OF PRODUCING A better model for development than the Manchester-Pittsburgh-Essen-Kharkov-Nagoya example offers. In Maoist terms, urban concentrations with large factories using sophisticated technology represent one "leg" of the policy of "walking on two legs". The other leg is small-scale rural-based industry. The urban leg, as indicated in the last chapter, is to be kept from growing too large and overcrowded, and cities will be distributed over the country as a whole rather than concentrated in only one area. But it is the small-scale rural alternative to urban-centered growth which has principally caught the imagination both of Chinese revolutionaries and of outside observers. Such a design seems to fit the circumstances, needs, and values of a peasant and village-centered China in both its traditional and its revolutionary setting; it also appeals to Chinese, and to outsiders, as a far more attractive path to development than is offered by grimy, de-humanizing, overcrowded cities. Perhaps the Chinese can indeed chart a better course.

Economic considerations, even speed, are not everything. As Mao himself put it, "People are the most precious things. It is

Man that counts." The *only* acceptable goal of economic development is to create a better life for people. That involves a great deal more than merely economic measures or graphs of production; it includes some consideration for the *quality* of life, not merely the quantity of goods. The Western-Japanese-capitalist concept of GNP as the chief measure of growth is both faulty and undesirable. China does not need electric can openers or color television, or huge cities merely because they are the cheapest or quickest way to accelerate the rise of GNP. Technology is not a god, nor an end in itself; it must serve the real and whole interest and the total welfare of real people. China is anxious to pioneer a new solution to the problems of development, one which is distinctively Chinese, suited to China's circumstances and worked out by Chinese innovation, not merely a copy of the discredited and distrusted imperialist West or of the samples of the Western model represented by the treaty ports. "Self-reliance" has been the watchword of the Chinese revolution, a blend of new national pride, rejection of foreign models, and determination to use the power of the mass line to create a wholly Chinese answer to China's needs, better for China but also better as a universal model for the rest of the world, which in the past acknowledged China's superiority for so long. The peasants are the great reservoir of revolutionary energy and innovation; they must be used, but as the leaders of change and its chief beneficiaries as well as architects, not simply as followers or delayed recipients of trickle-down from major urban centers. Indigenous methods and techniques, traditional and newly innovated, must be used to create human-oriented development rather than slavishly following the worn out and faulty example of the developed world whose failure in human terms is so clear from the Marxist perspective.

The Chinese are of course not the first to conceive of the small-scale rural alternative to urban concentration, nor even the first to attempt to pursue it. It is an idea which has appealed to a great many people, including planners, in many countries ever since the beginning of the industrial revolution. The excitement of the Chinese case is the government's commitment to this idea, and the power of central planning there, backed up by a revolu-

tionary ideology and drawing on the immense force of a uniquely
mobilized population, through the mass line. The bulk of China's
modern development still lies ahead; there is still time to plan a
better future, on China's almost blank paper. And as a still dominantly rural economy, it is in the rural areas that development
should ideally center, where in any case the main revolutionary
potential lies, in the peasant masses. Their energy is far more
likely to be tapped successfully if they can be involved in *creating* development themselves, from the ground up, rather than
acting on orders from the top down or serving as passive, delayed
recipients of a diluted version of urban-centered development.
The experience of all other developing countries makes it clear
that a grass-roots approach is far more effective in producing
growth and change, with local initiative and participation, than
change attempted from the top down or imposed from outside.

The economic arguments in favor of small-scale rural industrialization are also persuasive. Such enterprises fit the needs of developing countries especially well, since capital requirements are
relatively low: scarce and expensive capital can be substituted for
by intensive labor from the vast peasant pool. Local industry to
fill local needs saves transport, which is also chronically scarce
and expensive, especially in the amounts needed to move raw materials or distribute finished industrial goods. Small local enterprises can be constructed and brought into production very much
more quickly than can large centralized plants, and they make use
of what is often under-employed and in any case low-wage local
labor, thus contributing directly toward a solution to the ubiqui-
tous employment problem as well as enjoying relatively low labor
costs. Such enterprises also make use of local resources which
might otherwise be ignored or incompletely used, and they stimulate and draw on local initiative, galvanizing the rural people
into action toward modernization. Overhead and benefits' costs
are much lower than for urban workers, who must be provided
with housing, health and retirement coverage, child care and
educational facilities, urban transport, basic utilities, and so on.
All these things the rural workers supply for themselves: housing
in their existing family units, health care through the small an-

nual payments all must make to the rural commune system, old age security through dependence on the family or, if necessary, the production team (village-level sub-unit of the commune). As already suggested in Chapter 3, one of the most difficult problems of urban growth in poor countries is the inadequacy of housing and basic services, all representing costs which a developing country finds impossible to meet adequately; a small-scale rural alternative is thus even more attractive.

Most equipment used by rural small-scale producers is simple, small, and inexpensive; production is labor-intensive, perhaps only a little less so than traditional handicraft production. But there is a substantial net increase in output, at relatively low cost, and at the same time much labor time both newly employed, and freed (through the use of machines), for use in the intensification of agriculture or for other productive occupations. The best examples are probably the commonest rural production tasks: milling and processing of grains and other food products, and the spinning of cotton, both accomplished far more quickly, efficiently, and (overall) cheaply by simple machinery than by hand, as well as in far greater quantity. There are still in fact some labor shortages in Chinese agriculture, especially at peak seasons such as planting and harvest, so that changes which save or free labor can help to raise farm production and also enable more new irrigation construction or land reclamation. In calculating costs, however, one must bear in mind opportunity costs, i.e., the losses involved in foregoing alternative uses to which the same resources of labor and capital might be put. For most rural small-scale industry, opportunity costs are very low, since there are very few productive or viable alternative uses for the resources employed; most of what is produced is therefore in effect gravy. Finally, rural-based industry can make the most direct possible contribution toward reducing the gap between city and countryside, in standards of living and in overall culture.

Pursuit of such a rural alternative is however primarily a political decision in any country under any sort of government. Economic forces alone tend to concentrate industrial growth in large urban centers, for all the reasons pointed out earlier, especially since large investment decisions are commonly made by large concerns who are interested in maximizing and accelerating the return on their investment. This may be as true for states as for corporations, both of which are usually also concerned with large enterprises and accustomed to the economies of scale (the bigger the cheaper, including administrative and planning costs). The Chinese state is not only uniquely powerful, the agent of all planning, but at least in ideological terms committed to the ideal of rural development and to the rural small-scale approach. The Chinese state controls, or arbitrarily sets, all prices, allocates all transport, materials, labor, and technicians, and can thus pursue policy goals if it chooses to the disregard of normal economic constraints. After all, it is man that counts, or so the Maoist position reminds us.

Small rural industries in China are designed primarily to serve the needs of agriculture, which is recognized as the critical sector. Until it can produce large and consistent surpluses beyond the needs of current consumption (and remembering the still increasing population) all aspects of development remain in jeopardy. It is primarily agriculture which must create the surplus capital needed for industrial investment (and must pay for imported technology through exports), as well as providing an improved diet for China's billion people. So far, agriculture has managed in most years (the period of severe food shortages from 1959 to 1963 was a disturbing exception) to increase production only very slightly faster than population has risen, as far as both can be measured—admittedly neither very accurately. But the Chinese themselves acknowledge that agriculture is their critical problem, and for many Chinese, especially in less favored rural areas, diet or total food intake appears from some reports to be still marginal. The traditional farming system inherited in 1949 was highly labor-intensive and, by traditional standards, productive. This in itself makes it more difficult to increase output, since the system was already far from backward or inefficient; it had supported a huge population in relative well-being for many centuries. But it had ceased to produce significant surpluses, as population increased especially after the eighteenth century, and as nearly all potentially arable land was occupied and farmed. Labor intensiveness, and production, had bumped against a ceiling and agriculture could escape this trap only through an infusion of new technology. There is now very little new land which can be made productive, except at unacceptable cost. About two thirds of China's area is desert, semi-arid, or too cold or mountainous to sustain agriculture; and most of the pockets of new land which could be reclaimed by more modern technology have already been added to the system. Even so, the net contribution of much of this new land is marginal.

The bulk of increased output must come from existing cultivated land. But only a relatively small increase can be expected merely from increasing the already high traditional level of labor intensiveness, or from the consolidation of formerly tiny fields and the pooling of labor, equipment, and planning which the commune system accomplished in the late 1950's. New inputs of technology are needed: chemical fertilizers, improved crop strains, pest controls, better plows, tools, and machines, and large investments in increased irrigation—pumps, wells, dams, canals, piping, sprayers—all from the industrial sector. In return, agriculture could better supply industry with a variety of raw materials in addition to feeding China's people, providing some goods for export, and most important of all, creating surpluses for future industrial investment. Until the collapse of the Great Leap, the effort to have rural China lift itself by its own bootstraps, the state concentrated investment in the industrial sector and especially in heavy industry, following the Soviet model, in the hope that somehow better organization and more labor intensiveness through the mass line alone could solve the agricultural dilemma. Investment capital was scarce, there was not enough to go around, and industrialization was crucial.

The years 1959 to 1963 demonstrated that this was a formula for disaster. Traditional-style Chinese agriculture no longer had the capacity to produce surpluses or even to increase output to match population rises, which took place especially rapidly (unfortunately it is not known at precisely what rate) with the restoration of order in 1949 and the rapid improvements in public health. The Soviets had been able to draw on large Russian agricultural surpluses which China simply lacked. Beginning in the early 1960's, the Chinese state accordingly began to divert larger amounts of investment into production of inputs for the agricultural sector as the only possible strategy, even if this meant reducing the level of other industrial investment. Agriculture and industrialization are interdependent, but the most basic single need is for food. However, the urban-based industrial sector was still small, and it was necessary to walk on two legs in order to provide agriculture with what it needed from industry—hence the central role of rural small-scale plants.

Walking on two legs was officially defined as a balance of five relationships: industry and agriculture, heavy and light industry, large and small enterprises, modern and indigenous production methods, and centrally and locally run enterprises. The policy also specifically aimed to reduce the differences between mental and manual labor, workers and peasants, and city and country. The big cities must not grow bigger, and therefore new industrial labor should be absorbed primarily by small industries in rural and small town areas. Rural industry focused on what were called "the five smalls": cement, electric power, chemical fertilizers, iron and steel, and agricultural machinery. This sounds like a list of heavy industries, but it is also a list of the essential requirements of agriculture and the rural sector: cement for dams, irrigation channels, roads, and buildings; electric power for irrigation pumps and other agricultural machinery, and both household and industrial use; chemical fertilizers as the single most important need of agriculture for increased yields; iron and steel for local construction; and machinery (which also requires steel) to serve agriculture—tractors, plows, harvesters, threshers, carts, pumps, generators, and so forth. Some production of light consumer goods for local use was also provided for—textiles, clothing, processed food, furniture, utensils, and soap being instances—and some output of construction materials for local needs—bricks, tiles, lumber, and tools.

Each commune, and in many cases each production brigade (the middle-rank subdivision of the commune, a grouping of village-level production teams) was to have its own repair facilities for agricultural machinery plus some simple machine-making capacity. In a country the size of China and with its regional variety, including great disparities in local resources, leadership, income, and development levels, there are of course wide regional differences in all respects, including the degree to which official policy aims have been realized, but this was the approved design for all of China's 2110 counties (averaging about 300,000 each in population) and 74,000 communes (average commune population between 10,000 and 20,000). A key aspect of the effort to disperse development remains the transfer of technology, both vertically (from larger to smaller centers) and horizontally (among smaller centers), with the aim of evening out regional–local differences. Local technicians may be sent for short training or observation periods to larger centers, and urban enterprises are encouraged to share their knowledge and experience as well as to help build small plants in rural areas.

But the chief emphasis of the two-leg policy was on self-reliance in each locality, and on local initiative. This implied, as was also sometimes stated, that there was no intention to produce total equality of all places and regions. Some central funds were transferred, as in the case of Shanghai already cited, from more prosperous and developed areas to be invested in growth in more backward ones, but self-reliance was favored even while it was recognized and generally accepted that as a result areas which were already better off, and/or which made better use of their overall resource base, would develop farther and faster. The effort was also made to keep small- and large-scale enterprises, rural and urban spheres, distinct, not competing with or becoming substitutes for one another. Large-scale enterprises have remained almost exclusively urban, using sophisticated and capital-intensive equipment and producing for urban or even export markets, while rural small-scale plants produced largely for local needs. The two are further insulated from each other by the scarcity and high cost of transport linkages. But even without such a barrier, China is simply too big a country to make it feasible, even in pursuit of strictly economic objectives of rapid growth, to mo-

bilize and transfer labor, capital, and resources from all local areas
to large urban concentrations; to center all industrial production
there; or to distribute industrial goods with even minimal ade-
quacy from a few large centers even within each province (many
of them the size and twice the population of the major European
countries). When in addition there are policy goals to limit large
city growth, promote rural development, aid backward areas, and
reduce the urban-rural gap, the place of rural small-scale industry
would seem secure.

The only question is what its share shall be, what is the best or
most desirable balance between the two legs? And how is this
balance likely to change over time? That question has been answered differently at different periods. The first big expansion in
rural small-scale industry took place during the Great Leap
Forward between 1957 and 1959, when unfortunately a good deal
of it was poorly planned, hastily done, and unsuccessful. Much of
the iron and steel produced by the "back-yard furnaces", for example, was found to be of poor or even unusable quality. Rural
people were exhorted to produce industrial goods on their own
initiative and resources but given too little direction or support.
By 1960 there were about 60,000 small industrial enterprises
(many of them just workshops) at the county level and about
200,000 on rural communes. With the collapse of the Great Leap,
there were new pressures to make maximally efficient use of
scarce resources and to maximize output. In such a context, many
of the new small enterprises were clearly uneconomic or even
wasteful. Many of them used scarce materials—such as rubber,
plastics, finished steel and chemicals—and hence competed with
more efficient larger urban enterprises. These larger plants, with
more modern equipment, used far less fuel per ton of iron, less
iron per ton of steel, less fuel per kilowatt hour of electricity, and
so on. It also became clear that many of the funds and materials
for small rural enterprises had been obtained "through improper
channels" and diverted from official central plan allocations. As a
result of all these considerations, many small plants were closed
in the early 1960's.[25]

By 1963, with the qualified revival of the economy, a better based rural small industry sector began to grow again, and then boomed during the Cultural Revolution after 1966 with its radical return to the Maoist line. There was a particular expansion in the number of new small hydroelectric and iron and steel plants, and by 1972 there were some 35,000 of the former, which produced about 15 per cent of the national total hydro generating capacity. By that year, all provinces and all municipalities also had small or medium-scale iron and steel plants (not all of them by any means rural, however) which produced about a fifth of the nation's pig iron. There was also a very big increase in small fertilizer plants, using local materials, which by 1973-4 probably produced about half of total national output, although at widely varying levels of quality. Small-scale local cement plants, numbering about 3000, accounted by 1975 for perhaps 60 per cent of national production. For agricultural machinery and repair, to complete the "five smalls", there are fewer data but the general impression is that nearly all communes and all counties had by the early 1970's built some manufacturing as well as repair capacity, although for more sophisticated equipment—such as tractors, sprayers or generators—they were still dependent on large-scale urban plants. Controls had been imposed by the late 1960's to give procurement priority for scarce materials to large state and central projects and there was presumably less wasteful competition or duplication as a result.

But by the mid-1970's, it would appear that two of the "five smalls", fertilizers and iron and steel, had "almost exhausted the opportunities for further spread throughout the country"[26], and that these would shortly be followed by cement and electric power. One of the reasons was the growth by then, after a necessarily longer and slower development phase, of a great many new large plants in all four lines, some of them purchased in a package as part of the so-called "turnkey" deals whereby an entire factory is set up by a foreign contractor and his technical experts, who train local technicians, workers, and managers in the running of the plant, which is then turned over to its new owners. This was done particularly for chemical fertilizers. The government rightly saw an especially urgent need for major and rapid increases in fertilizers to boost agricultural output, and recognized that this could be done most effectively by importing whole large-scale plants and the foreign technology they encompassed. The small-scale rural plants were useful primarily to fill the gap in time until the large new plants got into production, after which it was assumed their role would sharply decline. Other new large plants were designed and built by the Chinese themselves, in a variety of product lines, but nearly all of this new investment, whether in domestic or imported industrial capacity, was located in urban areas, something which the size of the enterprises alone made rational. Some of these urban areas were largely new, and most were part of the dispersal pattern, away from the old coastal area and distributed more evenly among the provinces. But almost none were rural, let alone small.

It seems likely that small-scale rural industry in general reached its peak by the early or mid-1970's and may be expected to continue declining in terms of its share of total production, as new large (and urban) plants come on stream and as transport continues to improve. In most cases, the Chinese have found, as earlier experience in a great variety of places elsewhere also shows, that the economies of scale are real. Small-scale and rural production tends to be more expensive. In most cases its quality is also lower and in any case less uniform, since it uses local materials of varying and often low quality, less advanced machinery or technology, less skilled labor and management, and less standard quality control since it serves primarily a series of widely varying local markets. What keeps it viable, at least in strictly economic terms, is the transport cost barrier insulating local areas from major urban-industrial centers.

Cement is probably the best single illustration. The fragmentary data we have (cost accounting not being one of China's strong points) suggest that unit production costs for small local cement plants, most of which use standard but reasonably simple technology and equipment based on centrally planned blueprints to produce a single homogeneous product, are slightly higher than for large urban plants; output quality is uneven but often poor and in general far below the quality of large plant output, mainly as a result of low quality local materials—clay, limestone, coke, iron ore. But it may be adequate for many local needs, which are pressing especially in agriculture, and better grade cement from large urban plants is simply not available anyhow. Urban output serves the more demanding urban market, or goes into major projects such as large dams or large construction projects where high quality is essential. In any case, cement (like its raw components) is exceptionally heavy, bulky stuff and transport costs are thus excessive, particularly since cement and components have a relatively low value per unit of weight. This alone is likely to keep small-scale rural plants operating more or less indefinitely, although their role seems certain to decrease as transport improves and transport costs accordingly come down.

Local materials and labor are also the basis of most small-scale rural fertilizer plants; most of them too are built to standard designs furnished from the national level and use technical equipment provided from the modern urban sector, since the manufacturing process is rather more complex than for cement. Unit production costs appear to be significantly higher for most of these plants than in the new large fertilizer factories, and quality of output, though varying widely, much lower. Presumably they too will continue to decline relatively, as more large plants enter production and as transport improvements create a more national market. For iron and steel, small rural production appears to be very much higher cost than for large urban plants (not very surprisingly) as well as much lower in quality; small plants are also said to use almost twice as much coke per ton of output. Already by 1972 such plants had dropped to about a ten per cent share of national steel output (although it is not easy here to sort out, from the data available, small from medium-scale plants and rural from urban), which has probably since declined still further for the same reasons as in the cases of cement and fertilizer. The small rural iron and steel plants which survive in the longer term (if any) will presumably be those which happen to be close to high grade local deposits of ore and coking coal with low extraction costs. Local power generation—hydro and thermal—and farm machinery repair (plus perhaps simple equipment and tools) seem far more likely to retain at least their present absolute levels, but their relative role can only decline as larger and more cost-efficient plants continue to grow and distribution facilities improve.

None of this is to say that the investment in and boom development of rural small-scale production roughly from 1957 to 1975 was a mistake. Indeed it played a vital role, and probably saved China from near-catastrophe during the necessarily long time (further delayed by the Great Leap, the Cultural Revolution, and other policy shifts and inconsistencies) required to plan, build, and operate larger urban plants and to improve distribution. Even the Great Leap experience was not wholly wasted, partly because anyone learns from errors and partly, as Mao intended, because it provided invaluable first experience for millions of peasants, necessarily one of trial and error, with the process and problems of industrialization, as well as with the potentials and the limits of the rural context and its resource base. One can also argue that one of the chief purposes of the now declining small-scale sector is to train and provide experience for workers and technicians who will then be needed as the bigger and more efficient plants continue to expand. One could even justify them, following Sigurdson, as "pre-investment studies". Meanwhile, they have also added to local rural income and employment, and contributed vital goods to rural development in general and to agricultural growth in particular. It is largely thanks to the roughly 50,000 small local power stations that most communes now have some electric power, even if not yet all production brigades, teams, or houses. Although many poorer and more remote areas still lack power, one of the things which strikes a foreign observer is the extent to which electricity has been distributed in many rural areas, mainly from the small local power stations which are a feature of most communes. I personally see it as a symbol of the commitment to mass welfare and to rural needs. There is often only enough power to light a single low-watt bulb, or perhaps to run a radio, but on many communes this much is provided to most houses, perhaps as a promise that mass rural welfare has not been forgotten in the national drive for industrial growth and that even if the emphasis is now shifting to larger urban production bases the effort will be to make the results available to everyone, including rural areas.

The precise dimensions of the balance between urban and rural "legs" in the drive for development are very hard to measure, in the present or past, let alone the future. The data we have do not adequately distinguish small from medium-scale (and do not define exactly what is meant by either label), or more importantly for our purposes here, often do not distinguish rural from urban plants (there too there is lots of ambiguity about what is "urban"). But it is clear that many supposedly rural enterprises are far from small, and many small enterprises are in unambiguously urban areas with populations up to 200,000, or even in the big cities. Of all so-called rural industrial plants, about 40 per cent are county-level enterprises, usually in towns or small cities, and employing 50 to 250, or as many as a thousand, workers. Rural areas which are part of the three large urban administrative zones of Shanghai, Tientsin, and Peking contain 20 per cent or more of the total national labor force in what is classified as "rural" industry. Many poorer or more remote areas have no local industry at all, or only a token amount. Even in Hopei (*Hebei*), an east coastal province which is in general one of the most highly developed and which also contains Peking (the capital) and Tientsin (the third largest Chinese city), both major industrial bases, sample data suggest that less than 5 per cent of the total rural labor force is engaged in industrial production. Sigurdson suggests a national average of perhaps 2.5 per cent, which even so includes county-level enterprises—a far cry from the Maoist vision of a rural path to industrialization and an industrialized countryside. Even a commune near Peking had only 4 per cent of its labor force in all forms of industry (including construction, mining, road building, repairs, carpentry, and traditional handicraft production such as wicker baskets and straw sandals) in 1971.

Unfortunately, most of the available data deal with official policy or even slogans rather than with precise information about implementation. Most of the more specific accounts deal with what are clearly—and sometimes admittedly—model areas; some seem even like Potemkin villages, an impression many foreign visitors receive from their conducted tours of communes. Even the official line however has begun to change. The American delegation which went to China in 1975 specifically to study small-scale rural industry was told "There is nothing beautiful about small scale". (Had they read E. F. Schumacher's *Small is Beautiful?*) "What we need is *growth*". The Chinese freely acknowledge, especially in recent years, that they would be better off if they had a "modern" urban sector adequate to produce all they need and an adequate transport system to distribute it. Their main hope for the rural leg is that some of it can be made efficient enough to expand competitively, become "modern", and build large plants which will then stimulate urban growth around them. Other less efficient rural industry (probably most of it) will just fade away.

It is possible that strategic-military considerations may also influence Chinese efforts to avoid excessive urban concentration of industry. There is certainly no question of China's fear of the Soviet Union and of Soviet power to destroy Chinese cities by nuclear attack, against which there can be no effective defense. Tension between the two states has been high ever since the Sino-Soviet split in the late 1950's, and has periodically erupted into border clashes. During the late 1960's and early 1970's enormous labor resources and even some scarce materials were expended to create extensive air raid shelters in all major Chinese cities, especially those north of the Yangtze River and hence nearest to the Soviet border, but of course all of China is within easy range of Soviet missiles and bombers. Urban dispersal, to centers distributed around the country as a whole, lessens the risks somewhat, but rural-based industry in thousands of smaller centers could reduce strategic vulnerability still further. It seems clear however that the latter would also critically slow down the rate of industrial growth (and its level of technical sophistication), which would hamstring especially the strategic industries. A more rational perspective would urge China not to attempt the hopeless task of contesting with the Soviet Union in military terms, and to rely for its defense on the guerrilla strategy which

proved so successful against both the Japanese and the Kuomintang. But military and strategic policy is by its very nature, in
any country, the supreme irrationality, one which China is no
freer from than the rest of us. China's attitude toward the Soviet
Union may in fact be called paranoid, even though it is reasonable
enough to be frightened of so powerful and immediate a neighbor
and one with whom relations are already so bad. In trying to balance the advantages of dispersal, especially to rural areas, against
the pressures for rapid growth in the light of strategic considerations, the Chinese seem to have come down firmly on the side of
continued and increasing urban concentration.

Although the urban giants are, at least for the present, controlled in their growth, industrial output there continues to rise
rapidly. More significantly for our purposes here, large (as opposed to giant) and intermediate cities are growing very fast,
both in total numbers and in individual populations. Some of this
new urban growth will continue, perhaps increasingly so, to be
fed by sub-contracting in which small plants provide components, as some communes near the large cities already do. This is
a pattern which has long proved important and efficient in many
countries, most notably in Japan. But the Great Leap showed the
folly of trying to push modern industry to the village level, and it
was clear from the beginning, in China as elsewhere, that traditional handicraft industries, village-based or otherwise, can never
produce industrialization or the development necessary to break
through the poverty barrier. Basket weaving and homespun cloth
just won't do it, whatever their undeniable virtues. It takes steel,
concrete, chemicals—new technology and new energy—from
which can also come more food, medicines, hospitals, housing,
and eventually affluence. For China's billion people, huge
amounts of all these things are needed, a task wholly beyond the
powers of village industry. Regrettably, it would seem that the
only way to produce what is needed, at least at bearable cost even
for a revolutionary society which recognizes the importance of
non-economic values, is through large urban factories. If mass
welfare is uppermost, cities seem an unavoidable price which
must be paid for ensuring and enhancing it.

The Chinese now divide urban places into four categories:

1. commune or market towns from 10,000 to 20,000 population;
2. small cities, up to 200,000 (including most county capitals);
3. secondary or intermediate cities, up to one million;
4. metropolitan centers, over one million (of which there are now more than 20).

Categories 1 and 2 are designed to provide goods and services primarily to surrounding rural areas. In category 3, other industrial activities become more important than those related directly to agriculture. Heavy industry is concentrated in category 4, together with government and commerce. Industrial decentralization is, interestingly, defined as moving industry out of category 4 cities into *any* of the other size centers. Needless to say, none of the categories could be called rural. The Chinese are attempting instead to develop a better balanced urban hierarchy, in an appropriate spatial pattern to cover the country and its population as a whole. This seems without much question to be by far the best strategy, better certainly than overconcentration of development in a few huge cities on the margin spatially, and better also than attempting to move industry into rural areas.

All developed economies have evolved a balanced network of urban places of different sizes which are both cause and effect of development. It is characteristic of most developing countries, including China, that the urban hierarchy is top-and-bottom-heavy: a few giants with a disproportionate share of city population (and usually also clustered on or near the coastal edge of each country), and a multitude of villages and small market towns, the latter barely urban. The spaces of the hierarchy in between these extremes are inadequately filled. This is obviously one measure, and an important cause, of the urban-rural gap; there are too few bridges between existing urban and rural worlds such as a mature urban hierarchy could provide. Cities of small and intermediate rank and functions in the hierarchy can be the most important single factors in the diffusion of innovation from "modern" to traditional sectors, as well as direct transmitters of new technology to agriculture and improved services such as health and education to the population as a whole. Without them, development moves out spatially only slowly and incompletely. It is the nature of a mature urban hierarchy to form both vertical (between top and bottom, large and small) and horizontal (to like-size places) linkage systems and thus to make available to all areas a wide range of urban-based goods and services. At the bottom of such an urban hierarchy, the small market towns make an effective link with rural areas and rural people, but they need to be connected through an urban continuum vertically and horizontally.[27]

There are indications that the Chinese have, especially since the mid-1970's, turned their attention to this problem and have begun planned efforts to fill in the gaps in the continuum. Again we lack adequate data, but samples from Honan (*Henan*) province obtained by the American small-scale industries delegation in 1975 produce a picture which may well be typical of perhaps the more populous half of the country, judging from a variety of accounts in the Chinese press. The intermediate-size city of Hsinhsiang (*Xinxiang*) in northern Honan was said by local officials to have grown from some 57,000 in 1949 to 420,000 in 1974, based primarily on new factories, and six or seven other cities of similar rank in Honan were said to have had a parallel growth pattern. Chengchow (*Chengzhou*), the provincial capital and largest Honan city, had however been kept relatively constant since 1958 at between 700,000 and 900,000[28], according to the same officials. The signs of rapid growth showed in the intermediate cities: an acute housing shortage and many sub-standard units, streets in bad condition, lack of the tree-planting which is such a pleasant feature of most older and larger cities, and so on.[29] But these are presumably just the familiar and inevitable growing pains of development everywhere: the early stages are always difficult and even unpleasant. There seems little question that the major Chinese development strategy is now firmly committed to urban-based industrialization. This is already reasonably well dispersed spatially, and more recently with what seems like appropriate attention to filling in the previously empty spaces in a graduated urban hierarchy which can provide vital linkages for the diffusion of development. The rural small-scale alternative is fading, like perhaps other aspects of the original revolutionary vision, as China confronts the hard economic realities of development. What will the new, urban China be like?

5. Planning for a New Urban China

IT IS REALLY NOT POSSIBLE TO GET A COMPLETE OR COHERENT picture of urban planning in China. We have only a few partial samples of plans, and few specific descriptions of what urban planners intended except in the most general terms. We do not know in any detail what trends and changes have operated in planning circles over the past thirty years. In fact, we do not really know who the "planners" are, or whether there is a recognized branch of urban planning represented in the administrative structure or in the universities. There is certainly economic planning, and there has certainly been attention within that effort to the spatial arrangement of urban functions and services, and to the planned dispersal of cities over the country as a whole. Since that is the essence of urban planning, perhaps it is enough to answer our question, but it is difficult to say more. Planning decisions have clearly been made, and on a very large scale, but it may well be that many or most of them have been made by officials who thought of themselves simply as that rather than as "planners", their function being merely to carry out national policy at the local level. It does seem clear that until the late 1950's the Chinese paid special attention to the Soviet experience in this as in many other fields, and adopted many of their most important programs, for example functional zoning within cities. It also seems clear that the Cultural Revolution seriously disrupted urban planning and may have stopped or even reversed some earlier trends.

What we can perhaps most usefully do however is to provide a survey account of cities and urban planning now, or in the period since 1972 when there was a sudden and enormous increase in foreign (including American) visiting scholars and a consequent increase in information. It is still woefully incomplete, and much of it is impressionistic, based on brief and possibly unrepresentative observation. But it is perhaps enough to provide a general picture of what has been accomplished as of the end of the 1970's, a picture which can be compared at least in general terms with China's revolutionary goals to re-make the city in its basic nature, to correct its Western-inherited flaws, and to transform it into a fitting home for a new socialist man.

China already has, despite its relatively low level of urbanization—approximately 20 per cent of its total population—probably the third largest city population in the world, after the U.S. and the U.S.S.R. It needs to be pointed out again however that we have only fragmentary population data from China. We do not know for sure what the total population is, or its growth rate since the last official census in 1953. A total population figure of 958,230,000 (including Taiwan) and a current annual net growth rate of 1.3 per cent were announced at the National Peoples' Conference in Peking in June of 1979[30], but without indicating the nature of the sample data on which these were based, except that it was clearly not the result of a national census. A guess at the overall growth rate since 1953 can of course be made by comparing this figure with the 1953 census total of 591,000,000 (which also included Taiwan), but although the new total is certainly plausible it cannot be regarded as a hard figure. No city population figures were given in the announcement. The Chinese now say they hope to conduct a national census in 1981, and to reduce the net annual population growth rate to 1.0 per cent by or before 1985.

However, the "urban" category also remains ambiguous. Some official sources, including a definition issued by the State Council in 1955 (since the 1953 census had neglected to do this), have indicated that "urban" places include all seats of People's Committees above the county level regardless of population size, all places of 2,000 or more which are at least 50 per cent non-agricultural, and places between 1,000 and 2,000 which are 75 per cent non-agricultural (however this is determined).[31] Many, perhaps most, of these small settlements are probably better labelled villages rather than cities, but in any case we do not know precisely what proportion of total "urban" population they contain. Other sources, including atlases published in China in the 1970's, do not provide further breakdowns for settlements under 10,000. In addition, most cities, and especially the three large separate administrative areas of Shanghai, Peking, and Tientsin, include large numbers of agricultural workers and agricultural areas.[32] We do not know for most cities how much of the municipal area or population is urban and how much rural, although this seems to be most ambiguous in the larger cities. Unfortunately, city authorities also seem relatively vague and unconcerned on this point, something apparently typical of the disinterest in or naïveté about statistics in China, as well as their dearth. Urban population categories may well also have been applied inconsistently at different times, and there were long periods, including the aftermath of the Great Leap and the Cultural Revolution, in which the entire statistical system was disrupted. But it has never been highly developed and one is dependent for most data on chance (and often contradictory) references in the Chinese press over many years. Field observations by foreign visitors are hardly an adequate substitute, and in any case it seems clear that municipal officials are no better informed than the central government, in the absence of any regular or effective census system.

By piecing together what data we have, it would appear that there are approximately 24 cities over one million, about 25 between half a million and a million, about a hundred between 100,000 and 500,000, and something over a hundred from 50,000 to 100,000. All but the largest cities seem to be growing more rap-

1. Nanking Road, a major street in Shanghai, showing both Western-style buildings left over from treaty port days, and some newer shop fronts. Note the combination of bicycles, trucks and pedestrians, plus the overhead wires for electric-powered busses.   PHOTO: C.W. PANNELL

2. Urban landscape, Canton. Like most Chinese cities, nearly all buildings here date from before 1949 but there are a few newer multi-storey housing blocks. The black tile roofs are typical of traditional Chinese architecture.
PHOTO: R. MURPHEY

3. A newer planned city: Chengchow. Most building here is new, along wide tree-lined avenues with lots of space around most buildings. Functional zoning is responsible for the industrial clustering visible here, but also for considerable grouping of housing in association with employment.
Photo: *China Reconstructs*

4. Old-style urban housing, Kueilin. This is reasonably typical of perhaps half of the present housing stock in many Chinese cities, little changed since the revolution. However, newer housing blocks show in the background. Note also the bicycle.
Photo: R. Murphey

5. Crowded cities: Kunming. This was taken on a weekly market day, but could be duplicated on many days in any city or town in China.
PHOTO: R. MURPHEY

6. An old-style village on the outskirts of Canton. Houses and lanes are kept clean now, but both are otherwise largely unchanged since long before the revolution. The stone flags are necessary in this wet climate.
PHOTO: R. MURPHEY

7. Local industry: commune power station. This is a common sight on many communes, where local supplies of coal, or as in this case local water power, have been tapped by small-scale plants to provide electricity. PHOTO: R. MURPHEY

8. Local industry: commune steel plant. These workers are producing railway rails, with steel made in the same plant, from local bodies of ore and coal, all on a small scale. PHOTO: R. MURPHEY

9. New housing on a commune near Shanghai. These blocks contain small separate units for each family, and are of considerably higher quality than most commune housing.
PHOTO: R. MURPHEY

10. Old-style rural housing near Sian. These dwellings are partly dug out of the side of a hill, a common pattern in the hilly northwest and reasonably typical of most rural housing.
PHOTO: R. MURPHEY

idly than the small towns. Table I (page 81) lists what appear to be the 24 largest cities and gives population *estimates* for each. The chief goal of urban policy has been officially stated as transforming the cities from "consumers" into "producers". This is a reference to their supposedly exploitative past, especially during the treaty port period: " . . . it is only through the transformation of consuming cities into producing ones that the peoples' livelihood can be assured and also that urban construction can look forward to a bright future. This also represents the difference between socialist urban construction and imperialist urban construction."[33] Like so many official policy statements, this is almost meaningless. All cities, anywhere, are both consumers and producers, but for any city to exist it must provide more goods or services to wider areas tributary to it than it draws from its tributary area. Cities must generate their own support from somewhere; they cannot live simply by taking in their own washing. This was true even for the treaty ports; although some of their output was marketed abroad rather than in China, almost all of their industrial production (as opposed to processing of farm products) remained in China. One gathers from the larger context and from other references to this policy that it means additional emphasis on industry as opposed to trade, suppression of bourgeois "consumerism" and high life-styles, and re-orientation of city economies to expedite their serving of the countryside with both goods and services. But policy slogans and exhortations do not necessarily produce results, any more than they may describe plans precisely. The consumer-producer distinction, endlessly repeated, really does not help us much to discover either what urban planning proposes or what has been accomplished.

This is not easy to discover, in the absence of detailed published plans or surveys, but some picture can be constructed from press accounts and occasional interviews with foreign visitors. To begin with, national planning decrees, at least in theory, what kinds of industry and which plants shall be located in each city. Efforts clearly are made in this connection, and with a considerable degree of success, to control the growth of the largest cities, to spread new industrial development spatially around the

TABLE I
Urban Area Populations in China*

	1979	1953 Census**
Shanghai	5.8	6,204,417
Peking (*Beijing*)	4.4	2,768,149
Tientsin (*Tianjin*)	3.5	2,693,800
Shenyang	3.0	2,299,900
Wuhan	2.7	1,427,300
Canton (*Guangzhou*)	2.4	1,598,900
Nanking (*Nanjing*)	1.8	1,091,600
Harbin (*Haerhbin*)	1.8	1,163,000
Sian (*Xian*)	1.7	787,300
Chungking (*Chongqing*)	1.6	1,772,500
Taiyuan	1.5	720,700
Lanchou (*Lanzhou*)	1.5	397,400
Chengtu (*Chengdu*)	1.4	856,700
Changchun	1.4	855,200
Talien/Luta	1.3	766,400
Tsingtao (*Qingdao*)	1.3	916,800
Chengchou (*Chengzhou*)	1.3	594,700
Kunming	1.2	698,900
Tsinan	1.2	680,100
Hangchou (*Hongzhou*)	1.1	696,600
Changsha (*Qangxa*)	1.1	650,000
Shihchiachuang	1.0	373,400
Anshan	1.0	381,200
Fushun	1.0	364,600

* Left column lists my estimates, based on a variety of sources, primarily accounts in the Chinese press. These figures attempt to exclude rural populations included within the municipal limits of each city, but such calculations are necessarily guesswork.

It should be noted that with the exceptions of Shanghai and Chungking, the war-time capital, all these big cities have grown substantially, in many cases dramatically, in the 26 years since 1953. In these terms, the policy of controlling urban "giantism" has been at best a qualified success. In total, there were only nine million-class cities in 1953, as compared with 24 in 1979.

** The 1953 Census has been widely criticized, and these figures should be taken as indicating orders of magnitude only, despite the appearance of individual head-count accuracy.

country as a whole, and to promote the growth of smaller and intermediate centers, as already discussed. Each city in turn is supposedly divided into functional zones, distinct areas of different kinds of industrial production (with interdependent industries grouped together), commerce, or transport. Housing and service facilities for the workers associated with each are supposedly located adjacently. This pattern is derived to some extent from earlier Soviet styles of urban development, as the Chinese acknowledge, but seems to have been carried farther in China. To some extent, it may approximate at least part of the purpose of the original urban communes, established as a result of the Great Leap but subsequently abandoned, or reduced to the form of neighborhood workshops which still survive. The present planned housing units and workers' communities are however based largely on the presence of a major industrial cluster or other work unit. Housing is provided within easy walking or biking distance, and usually in large and often dreary blocks, although sometimes, in the largest cities, in a cluster of smaller communities with buildings we might describe as town houses, as in parts of Shanghai.

Most such areas are also provided with a full range of services: schools; health clinics or small hospitals; day-care centers for the young children of working mothers; shopping centers for vegetables, fresh fish and meat, dry, canned, preserved and other foods, clothing, household equipment, and so on. There is sometimes also a cinema or even a savings bank, run of course by the state. Urban wages are high enough for some that savings are possible for a few, especially when, as is common, all adult members of the family work, with aged parents (who still normally live with their children) as built-in babysitters, shoppers, and house-tenders. Even in Communist China, savings deposits pay interest. A park and other recreational facilities complete the self-sustained complement of each area. It all seems vaguely familiar to a Western observer, especially the "workers' villages" around the periphery of the still recognizable central business district of Shanghai. Foreign visitors to Shanghai are told that some 150 such work-housing complexes have been built there since 1949, about a third of them encompassing over 50,000 square meters each, which is considered large.

A number of Western elements are however missing. Housing is strictly functional, and although adequate (some observers have compared it favorably with the average quality of Soviet urban housing blocks), the space allotted per person and per family seems spartan by Western, though not by Chinese, standards. It is far more so in most urban housing outside the new blocks, including the still large number of housing units left over from before 1949, many of which are in poor repair. Housing remains perhaps the most critical urban problem in China, as in cities throughout the developing world. Chinese urban population densities have however always been notably high, probably higher than anywhere else in the world with the possible exception of the largest Indian cities. They cannot now be measured accurately enough, in the absence of adequate census data, to warrant giving figures, but Chinese urban density is beyond question. This also puts enormous pressure on other urban services: water, heat, light, sewers, schools, hospitals, and transport. None are adequate yet to satisfy demand (however that may be measured); but they are nevertheless clearly well above rural levels.

Although houses may be, and many are, privately owned (unlike apartments in the large blocks of workers' housing), one does not see privately owned lawns or gardens, but communally maintained green spaces and plantings. In many such urban areas one also sees fairly extensive plots or even fields of grain or vegetables, some apparently run on the same system as the private plots on rural communes cultivated by each household, with the right to consume or sell the produce on the open market, but others clearly managed on a collective basis with the produce considered as part of the total work output of the unit. Many urban houses and apartments, perhaps most, have a radio and a bicycle; many have a sewing machine or a camera; and some, at least in Shanghai, are provided with flush toilets and a one- or two-burner gas cooker. On a national basis most cooking, even in urban housing, is still done traditional style with wood, charcoal, or coal. But all of this probably represents some improvement in living standards since 1949 for most Chinese, who also have no basis for comparison with living standards in other countries.

Nevertheless, housing, food, clothing, and other essentials are still clearly not adequate to meet even the modest demands of the Chinese population, whose numbers have increased so rapidly since 1949, nor to keep pace with rising expectations. Except for the newly-built areas around their peripheries, including the new workers' housing, most of the cities still look very little changed physically from what they were like before 1949, including perhaps the majority of housing. It is possible that the *per capita* share of housing space in many cities has not increased significantly since then, especially given the rapid growth of urban population. The state can if necessary postpone investments in housing in favor of what are seen as more pressing needs (as the Soviet state has done) except perhaps where it is essential to attract or to provide accommodation for new workers at new industrial sites. But the best indication of the acute shortage of new (post-1949) housing is that it is still allotted by assignment, or in effect rationed. Housing space is probably scarcer, and for most people probably also less adequate in other respects, in the cities than in the villages (now referred to usually as production teams on rural communes). There too, most villages look physically very much as they did in the 1940's; they are much cleaner, free of flies and refuse, and with perhaps a new building or two to house team administrative offices, but peasant houses and lanes are largely unchanged. The main differences in rural settlements are at commune (sometimes brigade) headquarters, often in a small market town, where there is usually a school, a clinic or hospital, some small industrial enterprises, and often some new housing blocks. But the cities are far more crowded, and have grown much faster. Urban housing shortages are after all not surprising, but they are a reminder that China confronts the same set of problems, and to the same degree, as other developing countries.

In addition to housing, most other essentials are scarce in the cities, and are therefore rationed: rice, wheat flour, noodles, bread, cooking oil, and meat (where the ration is extremely small, even by Chinese standards—one kilo per person per month in Peking, the largest ration, 8 ounces in Harbin and Kunming). Poultry, eggs, and fish, like vegetables, are sold on "free" markets without ration coupons, but are often not available or are exorbitant. Sugar, bean curd (which is chronically scarce and for which there are long queues whenever it is available), cotton and other fabrics, bicycles, radios, hardware, soap (2 cakes per person per year), toothpaste, light bulbs (with only 40 watt bulbs or less available—an obvious means to save power), coal for household cooking and heating, cooking pots, and furniture are also rationed. The allotment of cotton cloth, a basic item especially in China, seems totally inadequate and ration coupons are in great demand so that they are often traded or sold on the black market at high prices. Except on the black market, where both scarce goods and stolen, traded, or counterfeited ration coupons can be bought, prices are fixed and there has been little or no inflation, but this is of little help if the desired goods are simply not available or insufficient.

Bicycles are also in great demand, especially given the shortage of public transport in most cities, which one can judge from the enormous size of the bus queues and the need often to wait to get on while three or four busses clear the stop. Yet essential as bicycles may therefore be, other industrial needs are considered still more pressing. Bicycle production in 1977, for example, was said to be only six million units, probably much less than half the annual population increase. The June 1979 announcement of the National Peoples' Conference gave 1978 output as 8.5 million, still well below annual population growth. There are also understandable complaints that bicycle prices are set at too high a level, four or five times the average monthly wage for most urban workers. Ownership, even in the big cities, where bikes are most needed, seems to be still less than one per family. When all adult members of most households work, and where despite functional zoning there is often also a considerable journey to work, this can impose severe hardship. Television sets, still a rarity, are also rationed, but there are frequent stories of well-placed individuals who have managed to acquire one (and somehow to pay the very high price, especially in relation to average incomes), usually through connections (as the Chinese say, "through the back door") or on the black market. It is discouraging that ownership of a television set has already become the biggest single status symbol. Public transmission is limited to a few hours each day, and until recently consisted of pretty dreary official news and propaganda films for the most part, but to own a set marks one as important. The government has now begun to transmit a somewhat more varied programming, including a few features of foreign origin, but status is the thing even in the Peoples' Republic.

It is clear that although the Chinese emphasize a complete form of urban planning, and have successfully accomplished a good deal of it, especially in the newer cities and newly-built areas around the older ones, it is in fact far from complete. As Western, Indian, and Japanese planners know to their sorrow, it is a gargantuan task to re-design (let alone to design) a large city which already exists and where there are a host of competing and often irreconcilable pressures, needs, and trends, not to mention group or individual preferences. One of the chief advantages of the functional zone system, with workers' housing, services, and shopping areas all adjacent to employment, is that it reduces commuting, at best a wasteful process which contributes also to congestion, pollution, unproductive use of energy, loss of work and recreational time, and de-humanization—all problems necessarily associated with most cities. Functional zone planning in most Chinese cities has certainly lessened the useless journey to work, but one has only to watch bus, bicycle, and foot traffic to realize that there is still a great deal of waste movement. Bus services run far behind demand, and there is an immense cloud of bicycles, which probably account for the majority of intra-urban movement beyond easy walking distance. Holidays or days off tend to be staggered as between different enterprises so that only a fraction of the work force is off on any one day, including Sundays, but even so there seem to be no days and virtually no daylight hours except very early morning when urban streets, busses, parks, and public buildings are not jammed with people.

The private car is still absent, giving China an enormous advantage over all other industrial or industrializing societies in a number of important ways. This is not only because as a still poor country it could not produce adequate numbers of private cars for its population, but results from a planning decision to concentrate investment and production on essentials for economic growth and mass welfare and to de-emphasize unnecessary luxuries for private consumption. Television, where production of sets is still very small, is not really an exception, since it is a powerful medium not merely of propaganda but for the diffusion of innovation. As the mushrooming destructive effects of the private car have become clearer in the West and Japan, the wisdom (and good luck) of the Chinese decision have become even more striking. One hopes that the planners will be able to hold the line on this vital issue in China as industrialization proceeds (and China increases the exploitation of its huge oil reserves), to avoid the tragic mistake which the developed world seems bent on perpetuating. Chinese truck and bus production is growing rapidly, as it must, and there is a small output of cars for official use only. One can however see occasional official limousines with children peeking out from behind drawn curtains, presumably bound for a family outing; occasionally one also sees purely luxury cars, such as expensive imported Mercedes in bright colors, though they are rare. This may be merely a reminder that the Chinese are as human and fallible as other people and that the bourgeois, corrupting nature of urban-based elitism is a perennial problem, which will continue to need controlling.

Apart from the work-housing complexes, many of which are associated with newly-built "satellite towns" arranged along the outer peripheries of the large cities and usually specialized in a particular industry, such as the electronics district on the edge of Shanghai, urban populations are also grouped into defined neighborhoods. These are designed to implement self-government and local administration, but also to expedite mass mobilization and through it to further both national goals and the ideal of local self-reliance. Neighborhood and block committees are responsible for settling disputes, maintaining houses and lanes, and keeping order. They form the basic units of all other forms of local government and planning, including the local organization links of the Communist Party. They are responsible for controlling deviant behavior, but depend more on highly effective group pressure, in an old Chinese pattern, than on specific sanctions. This structure is what remains of the original urban communes established after the Great Leap to serve also as work units on the pattern of the rural communes. Some neighborhood workshops still operate, but most urban employment is now in larger factories or offices. Neighborhood units and committees however still shape individual and group behavior according to national norms and local directives. No individual is free from these constraints, even in seemingly trivial matters such as the internal cleanliness of houses or the play activities of younger children. Household trash and garbage (of which there is very little given the long-established Chinese habit of frugality) are placed in small orderly and segregated piles in the lanes for regular pick-up, and the lanes are otherwise kept free of debris. Chinese cities are clean and well ordered, at least by contrast with most cities elsewhere.[34]

Despite the overall stress on planning, neighborhood administrative organs seem to have little control over land use in their areas, especially vacant land which may exist, where city or regional planning needs may override local preferences or ignore existing patterns. Vacant plots may for example be used to construct new housing blocks for workers in a different area, or other building which may have no relation to the local complex. On the other hand, old established neighborhoods may often not be provided by the planners with shopping or other services or with adequate transport connections to such facilities. The Cultural Revolution years tended particularly to neglect urban services, and by no means all of the gaps have been filled in since. The neighborhood workshops which survive from the urban communes engage in a variety of small-scale production, most of it designed to supplement and complement large urban plants. Since about 1960 they have employed primarily housewives, grandparents, and other previously unemployed or under-employed people, often on a part-time basis. There is a particular emphasis on the use of waste and scrap materials, but in general a very wide range of goods is produced. Larger projects of urban improvement, such as construction of new sewage facilities, cleaning up old stream beds, removing former city walls, constructing and maintaining new parks, and building new roads, are undertaken with labor drawn from neighborhood committees, factories, schools, and offices in the areas where the projects are located. Each such unit may assign a small part of its total labor force to the project for a set period, usually only a few days at a time, after which a new group of workers from other units takes over, so that work schedules of each production unit are not disrupted.

This all makes excellent sense; it uses otherwise underemployed labor and neglected materials to add to the drive for production, and also to create a better neighborhood and urban environment. Press accounts report that small neighborhood workshops in Nanking produce over a thousand kinds of items which in total are equivalent to the whole city's output of processed goods before 1949. Similar establishments in Chungking made fertilizer from tobacco waste and salvaged 100,000 tons of metals, chemicals, and other usable materials from waste materials. Family dependents of workers in Fushun (a large coal mining and industrial city in Manchuria) salvaged 50,000 tons of coal from slag heaps and discard piles; over 500 neighborhood workshops in Peking, staffed mainly by former housewives, used discarded or waste materials to produce a very wide range of industrial goods and accessories which comprised more than 10 per cent of Peking's total industrial output from district- and county-level enterprises; neighborhood processing stations for household trash and garbage in Shanghai extracted over 200 tons of usable oils for lubrication and 2,000 tons of re-usable rags and yarn.[35]

Schools everywhere operate as much as possible on the "half work, half study" system, although since the fading of the Cultural Revolution there has been increasing emphasis on study. However, most schools even at the elementary level maintain one or more workshops which are genuine producing units rather than simply training shops and which turn out goods for delivery to a nearby factory as components. The data we have do not make it possible to estimate how much of current total urban industrial production comes from small neighborhood units, but it seems unlikely to be a large share. Such efforts are good for morale, and of course every little bit helps in the urgent drive for growth. Nevertheless the emphasis in the cities, as in national planning as a whole, seems clearly and increasingly to be on large modern plants as the cheapest and quickest means of growth. Neighborhood workshops, like backyard steel furnaces or the more recent small-scale rural plants, are a useful temporary expedient and learning experience, but not for the most part an efficient long-run solution as development accelerates.

Cities are also to be transformed by correcting their effects in degrading the environment. China has an enormous advantage here in being still only slightly industrialized and hence able to plan prevention rather than attempting cure. The absence so far of the private car is also a priceless advantage. But the existing big cities offer immediate examples of the environmental dangers of concentrated industrialization, and the earlier Western, Soviet, and Japanese experiences are also available as object lessons. The Western case is in fact used to illustrate the tragic environmental consequences of the capitalist system, where the uncontrolled search for private profit leads to environmentally as well as socially destructive results.[36] One is however inclined to wonder if such views are still so prominent as China continues to pursue its own heavy industrialization, and primarily in urban concentrations. But the existing level of easily perceivable atmospheric and water pollution in Shanghai and other industrial cities is enough to sensitize the Chinese planners to the problem, fortunately before most of the country has gone very far along the same road. Smog in Shanghai is as bad as in many American cities, perhaps worse, but no measures are available for China.

Environmental degradation is to be corrected through industrial dispersal to smaller cities scattered around the country, as already discussed, and through a combination of cure and prevention. China cannot afford to scrap its existing industrial plants, but factories of older design (roughly before about 1965, when pollution control began to be considered as a policy problem) are supposed to be fitted with emission, waste disposal, and effluent controls. This is of course expensive as well as requiring new technological inputs. It is impossible to estimate how effective such controls have become or are likely to be. There are frequent accounts in the Chinese press of successful efforts of this sort, especially of those to make productive use of industrial wastes, but there appear to exist no general or adequate measures of overall effectiveness or of current or changing levels of atmospheric or water pollution. Many new enterprises, including neighborhood workshops, have been established using industrial discards or discharges as their basic raw materials; others reclaim wastes and return the resultant product to the factories. Electric busses are favored over internal combustion wherever possible, and some urban railway lines are also electrified although the chief locomotive fuel for trains as a whole is still coal, with diesel power rapidly overtaking it. The greatest progress in pollution control will clearly have to come from the design of new plants and the location of enterprises. Factories built since the late 1960's must include pollution controls (although no specific standards have been published) and make productive use of their own treated wastes. Industrial enterprises in any one urban area are supposed to be clustered in any case on the basis of interdependence but are also arranged so as to make use of each other's wastes.

Given the traditional importance of human wastes (nightsoil) in maintaining agricultural yields, this is not a new concept to the Chinese, and indeed there are a number of new projects in cities to channel urban biological wastes and non-toxic sewage more completely and effectively to the surrounding agricultural areas. Atmospheric and other industrial effluents which are not usable agriculturally are supposed to be prevented or trapped and where possible converted into re-usable form. Foreign visitors have been taken to see an early but advanced sample of a new model factory in the industrial zone of Peking suburbs where toxic discharges pass through successive treatments: each stage removes materials which can be re-used, by the same or other factories, and at the end of the treatment line is a small lake of clear water in which ducks and fish swim, for the supply of the factory canteen and for recreation during lunch breaks.

Planning also takes account of prevailing winds and attempts to locate nuisance industries where possible on the downwind side of urban areas as a whole. Previous haphazard location patterns have in many cases been corrected by merging similar plants and re-locating them in new suburban areas; related industries are grouped in distinct suburban zones, such as the electronics cluster outside Shanghai already referred to; other clusters at other points in this Shanghai-satellite suburban ring include chemical engineering, petrochemicals, metallurgy, and machine building. Each of these separate industrial centers is equipped with workers' housing, schools, a range of shops, parks, hospitals, and other basic services. There is also an emphasis, especially since the early 1970's, on closer economic interrelations between cities and their surrounding rural areas. Each municipal area (most of which contain considerable agricultural land) is to strive for self-sufficiency in vegetables, and where possible other food, while at the same time concentrating its own production on the provision of goods and services needed by its immediate hinterland. Industry and agriculture are to be interfingered as much as possible through suburban dispersal of many factories, and suburban or near-urban agricultural areas are to concentrate on growing food for the city of whose larger region they form a part. This obviously saves long-distance transport and involves other important economies, in both directions. Urban young people assigned to the countryside are increasingly being sent to communes in the vicinity of their city, to help further cement these rural-urban ties in perhaps a more lasting fashion than could result from shipping such people long distances away to different regions, and thus severing their urban links entirely as well perhaps as feeding the determination of many of them to return to their original city if they possibly can.

Whatever the shortcomings in practice of urban planning in

the larger and older cities, many of the new cities away from the coastal zone are much more completely planned and are described in the Chinese press as models of new-style urban development. This is especially the case with the wholly new major oil drilling and refining city of Ta Ch'ing (*Daqing*) in the Sungari Basin of northern Manchuria, not far from the older city of Harbin (*Haerhbin*). Ta Ch'ing is extolled as a model which all cities should follow, especially in its allegedly successful effort to eliminate the distinctions between city and countryside, industry and agriculture. It is a city of about half a million, but laid out over a very large area in which oil wells and refineries are widely scattered, interspersed with cultivated fields and small or medium sized residential areas. Ta Ch'ing is praised as an example of combining rural and urban, agriculture and industry, but also for its frugality and self-reliance in using local materials, especially pounded earth walls for houses and other buildings, and for its pioneering spirit, under the harsh subarctic conditions of northern Manchuria. The "city" contains three townships and three rural communes, with 41 "central villages", but there has been an effort to avoid the growth of any central business district. However, some of the refining of crude oil is done at the pre-existing county town of An Ta (*Anda*), some 80 kilometers away, and to that degree the normal amount of urban-industrial concentration at Ta Ch'ing may be less necessary. A great deal of the oil produced is also shipped out by pipeline to major refinery centers in southern Manchuria (at Talien, the major port) and in the Peking-Tientsin area, closer to the market.

Oil workers are also supposed to take some part in agriculture, and farmers and workers' wives run small factories on the neighborhood workshop model. Exactly how integrated these activities or roles are is hard to say, in the absence of detailed data on employment, production, or investment. We have only general descriptions of Ta Ch'ing as both "rural city" and "urban countryside". There is of course a major railway station and junction there, and it is not clear how possible it will remain to prevent some degree of commercial-industrial clustering around it. To some extent, the more usual problems of urban growth can be avoided in any primarily extractive center, most of whose output is shipped out in raw form for processing elsewhere. There may be relatively little normal urban development at oil extraction sites elsewhere in the world too. This alone suggests that the supposed model of Ta Ch'ing is not really applicable to urban planning problems in the rest of China, and certainly not to already established cities, not only those in the old coastal zone but the many others constructed in each province since the 1950's. As for self-reliance, it is a little puzzling that foreign visitors are told that despite its agricultural component Ta Ch'ing supplies only half or less of its total food needs—presumably a reflection of the harsh climate and very brief growing season. And despite the emphasis on "self reliance", there have necessarily been huge central state inputs of capital equipment in order to bring the wells and refineries into production and to keep them operating, as well as to construct the pipelines. Finally, it is hard to tell how successful Ta Ch'ing has been in avoiding other urban problems, especially environmental pollution and elitism. Foreign visitors describe it as one might expect an oil town to be: unsightly, smelly, and generally unattractive, with what American oil technicians who have seen it describe as very low maintenance standards. Its virtue in environmental terms is its relative isolation from the main population concentrations so that the pollution it generates is at least dispersed.

Elitism is a far more difficult thing to control. It is concentrated of course in cities, where managers, technicians, and professionals cluster. Early accounts of Ta Ch'ing praised the selfless virtue and hard work of model workers, especially "Iron-man" Wang, who went "all-out" in the fierce Manchurian winter to keep the drilling going and construct the facilities. The built-in link with agriculture at Ta Ch'ing and the use of industrial workers for farm tasks is also supposed to preserve and re-charge their "purity" and revolutionary vision. But as development proceeds, can even Ta Ch'ing keep specialist technicians, plant managers, and other white-collar types from acquiring greater prominence, and greater rewards? Rewards are necessary, even in a socialist system, to stimulate effort, and Communist China has never even tried to treat all people equally. There is a very wide range of wage and salary rates: high-ranking professionals (doctors, professors, engineers) are paid at the top about ten times the lowest wage for commune workers. And, not surprisingly, urban wage and salary rates average over twice those in rural areas. The June 1979 National Peoples' Conference announced the average annual income of industrial workers (overwhelmingly urban) as nearly ten times the peasant (rural) average. (These figures are admittedly a little hard to explain, although "industrial workers" and "peasants" were not further defined in the announcement and may represent, as categories, extremes rather than averages.) Higher income people naturally enough want to use their money to support a life-style which is better than those below them: better housing, better food, more consumer goods, and access to better education for their children so that they may become professionals too. These are the kinds of things, and the kinds of attitudes, which all cities everywhere generate. Even Ta Ch'ing is not likely to be a complete exception.[37]

Another model city, and probably more appropriate as an example of planning which is applicable more generally, is Chengchow (*Chengzhou*), the capital of Honan province. Before 1949, it was a small, backward, and unattractive town at a rail junction just north of the Yellow River. It has been almost entirely replanned and re-built, with broad tree-lined avenues. Housing, factories, and public buildings are spread out over a very large urban area in functional clusters, separated by green belts which are used for productive agriculture as well as for recreation. Chengchow's growth has been controlled, although as already suggested the data are ambiguous. What is even less clear is the extent to which urban elitism has been controlled. But Chengchow is undeniably a pleasant planned city which successfully combines the best aspects of functional zoning with an interfingering of agricultural, recreational, and industrial land use. As a largely new city, probably the majority of housing is new, and is certainly more nearly adequate in both amount and quality than in the larger and older cities, as well as being more completely integrated spatially with employment and with adjacent shopping, education, medical, and other service facilities. Sian (*Xian*), an old imperial capital and now the capital of Shensi (*Shanxi*) province, has also grown enormously since 1949 as a new industrial base. Perhaps two thirds of the present urban area is new since then; it has thus been possible, as at Chengchow, to plan its development, and along similar lines.

Other cities are, like Ta Ch'ing, wholly new and based on newly discovered local resources, such as the iron and steel city at Pao T'ou (*Baotow*) in Inner Mongolia. Pao T'ou makes a good illustration of national planning policy in that when a rich field of iron ore was found in the vicinity in the early 1950's, the decision was made to locate the iron and steel-making capacity there rather than hauling the ore to an existing industrial center or city closer to the center of the market and to supplies of coal. Pao T'ou was picked in part precisely because it was remote, so that industrialization there could accelerate the development of this previously backward region as a whole and could involve its people directly. The same approach underlies the boom industrial and urban development of distant Sinkiang (*Xinzhiang*): the chief urban-industrial center at Urumchi (*Urumqi*), now about a million in population, is nearly 1500 miles from Peking and considerably farther from the national center of population or production. Sinkiang contains rich reserves of oil, iron ore, coal, and other minerals, but the cost of shipping them to the major markets or industrial centers is very high. On the other hand, Sinkiang itself is mostly desert and the population is relatively small. In practice, the planners have attempted to make Sinkiang as self-sufficient as possible, producing its own industrial goods from local materials, but the unit costs of most production there are higher than in established industrial centers closer to the market. If rapid industrialization at least cost were the only goal, Sinkiang, Inner Mongolia, northern Manchuria, and most of China's western and northwestern provinces would be ignored, and development still concentrated in the east coastal zone. But the Chinese planners are quite properly concerned with more than strictly GNP-economic goals, although to what degree may vary over time. In the past couple of years the pendulum seems to be swinging increasingly toward an emphasis on growth *per se*, and away from self-reliance in favor of imported technology. But regional development is nevertheless still pursued for its own sake, as something axiomatically good whether or not it is slower and more expensive in terms of promoting the growth of GNP.

For the most part, the new socialist city in China is still more vision than reality. Much has certainly been accomplished through planning, and there are some notable successes: the satellite centers around Shanghai and Peking, largely new and planned cities such as Chengchow, new nuclei of industrial growth in previously remote areas such as Pao T'ou and Urumchi, and in nearly all the cities new complexes of housing and services grouped around new industrial clusters. Functional zoning, which seems to be adhered to as much as possible despite the difficulties presented by the larger and older cities already well formed before 1949, makes good sense and has clearly helped toward a solution of many basic urban problems. Some of the ideals of the commune and its emphasis on mass mobilization for common effort have successfully been transplanted to the cities in the form of neighborhood workshops and collective efforts at urban improvement. The success of efforts to control pollution is much harder to measure, but the problem is clearly recognized and at least a beginning made, perhaps much more, toward solutions both through regulatory restrictions and through locational planning.

More recently it has become clearer that environmental quality and its preservation have (and perhaps since 1949 have always had?) a lower priority than economic growth *per se*, especially when the two are in conflict, as they usually are. Soochow Creek in Shanghai is admitted by local officials to be "well below standard", whatever that may mean in the absence of published or available standards. Impressionistic observation by foreign visitors of water and air pollution in Canton, Shenyang, Tientsin, and other larger cities suggests that they may be as bad as Shanghai, and probably worse than the American or European urban average.[38]

The overall size of the largest cities has however been kept under control, and efforts made to disperse new industrial growth to new intermediate centers which are rapidly filling in the urban hierarchy as they fill in previously blank spaces on the map. But while these are all positive steps, they have at best eased somewhat some of the apparently inevitable pangs of growth. Chinese cities show—or perhaps would show if we were able to measure and to see them more completely—essentially the same problems, and perhaps to about the same degree, as are shown by most cities in the rest of the developing world: overcrowding, inadequate housing, and basic services of all kinds running far behind population needs. The parallel with the rest of the developing world is completed by the pressures which have recently become much clearer in China from people who want to move from the countryside to the cities, however overcrowded and inadequately serviced they are. The kinds of tensions implicit in these pressures are examined in the next chapter.

6. Tensions

PERHAPS THE MOST STRIKING ASPECT OF CHINA'S EFFORT AT
planned control of city growth has been the policy of assigning
urban people to work in the countryside. In the Chinese context
this accomplishes two purposes: it restricts the growth of urban
populations by siphoning off a significant part of the yearly increase, and it educates or re-educates urban people in "correct"
attitudes, kindling or re-charging their commitment to serve the
people, who are primarily in rural areas. Theoretically, at least
some urban people have acquired skills which may also be useful
in the drive to raise rural productivity, and their labor alone can
help. But more stress seems to be placed on the educative and
morally purifying virtues of productive labor in the countryside,
especially for city-bred people, in keeping with the peasant revolutionary origins and base of contemporary China. Cities breed
bourgeois values, and the only way to root them out, to cleanse
the poisons which city life generates, is to labor with the untainted peasants in the countryside. Such ideological remolding,
and the contribution which urban recruits can make to rural development and to the urgent drive for increased agricultural output, are the official reasons given for this policy, but it seems clear

that even more important practical reasons lie behind it: the need to limit city growth. Urban jobs are still not increasing anything like as fast as even natural city population growth rates. In addition, the cities cannot keep up with the consequent demand for housing, food, and basic services. Urban workers require all these things, and hence also contribute to higher industrialization costs in the cities. In the countryside, workers sent down from the cities as redundant can somehow be fed, housed, employed, and provided with traditional and commune-based forms of social security at little or no additional cost but merely absorbed into village and commune systems.

From the beginning of the revolution there has been a tradition of glorifying manual labor. This was further institutionalized in 1957, attendant on the Great Leap, in the practice known as "hsia-fang"—"sending down"—which involved the assignment of urbanites, mainly intellectuals, elites, and government workers (including party cadres) for a month or more each year to do productive labor in the countryside. Hsia-fang was designed to re-sharpen their revolutionary dedication and re-educate them in the realities of a predominantly peasant China. The practice still continues, although apparently as a declining gesture. It has all kinds of appeal; one is inclined to wish that it could be applied in other countries too. Hard physical labor is good for everyone; and perhaps especially if it can be devoted to the common good, for high-status urban people who too often forget the realities of life for the masses and the need for common effort in their own selfish pursuit of advancement and privilege. China's use of hsia-fang is of course a reminder of its still basically anti-urban bias. Even some high officials and many highly skilled professionals, such as surgeons and research scientists, do, or did, their time each year in the countryside, and many of them spoke very positively, even convincingly, about it. Many professionals may of course have skills which are of direct use in rural areas and can contribute importantly to rural development or immediate needs while at the same time remolding their own values. In the late 1950's, partly no doubt to try to correct the balance which had been upset by incompletely controlled migration to the cities especially during and after the Great Leap, very large numbers of urban cadres—perhaps two million by the end of 1958—were sent down to lower administrative levels in rural areas, supposedly for good. At the same time, the hsia-fang policy was extended to require *all* white collar personnel in cities to spend at least one month each year in physical labor in the countryside.[39]

Whatever the virtues of the hsia-fang system, and even if it were maintained on a significant scale, it can make only a very small contribution to controlling overall urban growth. It is perhaps significant that even before hsia-fang was institutionalized, a more permanent form of urban-rural population transfer was established. This is the "Shang-shan hsia-hsiang" movement ("up the mountains and down to the countryside"), launched in 1955 and still in effect, to assign urban secondary school and college leavers and graduates to rural areas *en masse*. Like nearly all programs it was disrupted by the Great Leap and the difficult years of retrenchment which followed. Up to 1966 about a million urban youths may have gone to the countryside under this program, but between 1966 and 1976 perhaps as many as 15 million were transferred. This is something like one tenth of China's total urban population, or probably not far from the total annual population increase.[40] Unlike the hsia-fang system, shang-shan hsia-hsiang aimed to settle urban youths permanently in rural areas, where they were to "strike roots firmly" and make their homes. Continual exhortation as well as pressure was exerted to mobilize those sent down, and Party members were often encouraged to show the way by sending their own children to agricultural villages. In some cities and in some years it would appear that entire graduating classes have been transferred in this way. The youths were often required to sign a "letter of determination" which affirmed their commitment "to strike roots in the villages and work there permanently".

The state pays the (one-way) travel and the first year's living expenses, which usually include the cost of any necessary new housing and the purchase of furniture and tools. Thereafter the transferees are on their own, paid by the rural commune according to the standard work-point system based on the amount and supposed value of each individual's labor contribution and judged by those in charge at the end of each major harvest or work period or at the end of the year. How much in fact these transferred youths contribute to rural productivity is not clear. Most of them have little training or experience which is directly applicable to agriculture, although a few may have learned some workshop skills. Primarily they contribute their labor, working alongside the peasants doing the usual manual tasks. They must of course learn the job, but the purpose of their assignment is not re-education in preparation for a return to the city, as with hsia-fang: that is still limited to older and higher-status urbanites, including those (mainly Party cadres) sent in the late 1960's and early 1970's sometimes for as long as a year, to the famous "May 7 Cadre Schools" (established by a directive from Mao on May 7 of 1966) to do physical labor and political study so that they may return to their jobs in the city with their attitudes "corrected". Following the Cultural Revolution, from 1967, one must also distinguish the relatively few people chosen to attend universities (where enrollments were sharply curtailed for several years), and who were selected only from those who had done two years of productive labor in the countryside, a condition particularly required of the children of urban elites or former entrepreneurs. But for the great majority of rusticated youth, their rural assignment was for life, or at best indefinite. There simply were not jobs for them in the cities, while they could at least earn their keep on the rural communes.

Some of these sent-down youths were former Red Guards, brought into existence by the millions in answer to Mao's call for revolutionary cohorts to shake up the self-satisfied *status quo*-ism which the Cultural Revolution was designed to correct. They disrupted universities, offices, and factories and even for a time occupied the Foreign Ministry and other major departments in Peking. Trains were comandeered to transport Red Guards from all over China to Peking and other large cities where they could carry out their revolutionary mission.[41] The Red Guards had their brief time of glory, but the mass disorder and large-scale violence, especially in the cities, which they were encouraged to create got out of hand, and in the end Mao reluctantly agreed to call in the army to suppress them. Many were rural youths who had flocked to the cities, but in any case a place had to be found for them, and shang-shan hsia-hsiang provided the obvious solution. One can understand that many of the Red Guards felt bitter about it, however, and felt that they had been betrayed. Others among the sent-downs were urban secondary or college graduates who had come originally from rural areas and who merely returned home on graduation. But school and college graduates, whatever their origins, were in some sense—and often in their own eyes—the cream of the society, potential elites, professionals, managers. Over half, and probably more like three quarters of those sent to the countryside under this program ended up doing only manual labor.

To many of them—and to their parents as well as other Chinese—it seemed a waste of their training and supposed talents, especially in a developing system where training is still scarce and there is a gross shortage of technical and managerial skills. The press reported nearly every week the gala send-offs and encouraging speechmaking which accompanied most shipments of young people from the cities, praising their determination and self-sacrifice in committing themselves to serve the peasants, and to learn from them. Some perhaps did go originally with some enthusiasm and some sense of dedication to what are after all by their nature infectious revolutionary goals, in an atmosphere of mass commitment. Others seem to have sought rural assignment in the knowledge that two years of it was now a pre-condition for admission to post-secondary education; still others—probably a majority—had sought but failed to find an urban job and accepted rural assignment in the absence of any alternative but with the hope that before long something might turn up for them in the city once they had done a respectable amount of rural labor. But there were surely very few who looked forward with any sense of expectation to a lifetime, or even to ten years, of shovelling manure or digging irrigation ditches on a commune, cut off from the varied stimuli and at least potential opportunities of the city with which they were already familiar. Whatever early enthusiasm they may have had for their model role soon faded for most.

Shang-shan hsia-hsiang has certainly helped to limit urban overcrowding and unemployment, and it has also had the effect of scaling down what were probably exaggerated career ambitions for young people. This may in fact be one of the most cancerous problems of the developing world as a whole, especially in its cities, where an army of educated unemployed grows bitterly and even dangerously disillusioned as the process of development moves too slowly to make what they consider an appropriate place for them, or obliges them to seek work which they feel is beneath them. A national ethic which stresses instead the need for, and the virtue of, manual labor in the countryside can thus make an important contribution. The June 1979 announcement of the National People's Conference gave a figure of 20 million unemployed in China, and acknowledged that half of them were urban. It is certainly true also that development is hampered and skewed when urban-trained technicians or professionals insist on remaining in the city and refuse to take part in the diffusion of change by going where they are most needed, in the rural areas where most people are and where the basic problem of agricultural modernization and village-level improvement must be tackled. Directives from Delhi, Peking, Djakarta, Tehran, or Lagos won't do it, nor will brief or ceremonial visits by city-based "experts". Change can be fully effective only from the ground up, but it must be aided by urban-trained technicians who are willing to work directly with the peasants, share their lives, and win their confidence. In this light, the Chinese strategy is excellent and has attracted enthusiastic attention all over the world. But human nature does not differ much from place to place. Personal ambition may vary, but for many, even in a revolutionary society with all its claims on self-sacrifice, the urge for self-advancement gets in the way of the national goal to serve the people.

This may be especially the case in China, where education has always been seen as the means to status improvement. The Maoist mistrust of urban elites thus runs counter to much longer-standing attitudes and values which gave special respect to education and which assumed that "men of learning" had both a right and a duty to lead. It is still expected, especially by most parents, that education should lead to higher status. Bernstein concludes[42] that the shan-shang hsia-hsiang program has produced little or no change in these attitudes, and that "mobilization for rustication" is extremely difficult, perhaps as difficult in China as anywhere, despite the pull of revolutionary enthusiasms. Extensive letters and stories in the Chinese press, and the 1973 investigation of the program, revealed massive discontent with it, as was perhaps only to be expected.[43] The program also too easily lent itself to abuses: it was used often simply as punishment, or to pay off old scores and political faction rivalries. Cadres, who are supposed to act as models for other people, often used their position to obtain exemption from rustication for their own children, who ended up instead in a city job or in a university. One of the worst aspects of the program was its unpredictability. Not all graduates were rusticated, nor were all sent great distances. It was hard to know who would be taken, or whether they would go to some remote province as opposed to a place from which they might at least visit relatives occasionally. The time involved—or as many put it, the length of the sentence—was also unpredictable. In almost no cases were people told how long they must stay except that they were enjoined to "strike roots permanently"; but some were able to return to an urban assignment after a year or two; others returned illegally; and morale among those who remained was often bad.

There were, predictably, serious adjustment problems for most of those rusticated—and for their peasant hosts, who often resented these outsiders for whom they had to make a place and who were often accused of "superior attitudes". They had few useful skills, many of them were or became resentful of their new lot, and they were treated often as irritating and unwanted burdens, which no doubt they often were. There were predictable problems about housing, life-styles, and social life, and often bitter feelings about dating between rusticated youths and villagers. Cases of violence and rape were reported. From the peasant point of view, it is wholly understandable that the costs and grief of the program far outweighed its questionable benefits, especially since the sent-downs had few usable skills, were unused to hard physical work, and were often chronic complainers. It was all perhaps predictable, but nevertheless a serious matter, involving perhaps as many as 15 million youths. They in turn tended to form a counter-culture, as also might have been expected, drawing in on themselves and nursing hopes that they might be able to return to the city. For the disgruntled, almost certainly a majority, the chief value change achieved by the program was an upgrading of urban manual labor, which now looked good by comparison with their rural lot. The program has also contributed to a change in class and status criteria, which has tended to become based less on occupation than on the distinction between rural and urban residence—hardly the result at which the program aimed. Very few of the sent-downs seem to have served as catalysts for change, as was intended, or were able to make any significant contribution to rural development. Bernstein suggests that only about 15 per cent were employed in any kind of even minor "leadership roles"; the great majority were reluctant, ineffective, and increasingly resentful manual laborers.

More recently, and increasingly from 1977, there has been more open controversy in the press about whether the program's goals are in fact realizable, and even questioning the goals themselves. Teng Hsiao-p'ing, before his restoration to power, had been accused of saying that the program was in fact an obstacle to modernization, and that what China needed most was more technicians, more education, as rapidly as possible, not the rural-based mass line. Shang-shan clearly interfered with advanced training, and Teng suggested that the ablest students should go directly from secondary schools to universities or technical training units. The employment crisis for trained people can best be solved by rapid urban-industrial growth which can create jobs. But no one has argued that rustication is a strategy for maximizing the national economic growth rate. Now that Teng is back in full power since 1978 and the pendulum seems to have swung

decidedly toward emphasizing large-scale national growth,
shang-shan may well be abandoned except perhaps on a small
window-dressing basis. The attempt may be given up, as many
have argued, to achieve the impossible task of transforming an
urbanite into a peasant or of persuading most people to sublimate
their ambitions for status improvement. There is certainly a basic
conflict within China's revolutionary goals: ideologically, they
aim to create a new socialist man, free of selfish ambition, but
they also emphasize economic development, which may require
an "economic man".

Official exhortations to "serve the people" are not likely to
change values permanently. Most Chinese, like most people anywhere, do not take full satisfaction from being, as they are urged
to enjoy being, "a cog in a machine". Like others, many of them
aspire to becoming a wheel, or a puller of levers. Mao cautioned
against young people "going to the countryside in order to become an official" or "to gild one's self," but that is exactly what
many of the sent-downs seem to have tried to make of their rural
assignments. And education is still seen as the vehicle for upward
status mobility, despite official denouncements of "studying to
become an official". No regime can happily accept—or perhaps
survive—the deep alienation and demoralization which the
shang-shan program seems to have generated. Nor can official
glorification of rural challenges dim the attractions of the city.
Ever since the Cultural Revolution the majority of those who
have become refugees from China to Hong Kong have been rusticated youths. It is significant that very few of them seem to have
had ideological motives for attempting this very dangerous solution; most of them swim out, braving armed guards, sharks, and
strong currents as well as severe penalties if caught. The risks are
dismaying, but they are not undergone out of anti-Communism
or even of negative feelings about the regime as a whole. The
issue for most of them is simply that rustication left them with
too little scope for their own career ambitions and that they pre-
ferred the risks of escape, back to the urban world, to an indeter-
minate sentence in the countryside. And these were of course

young people, some of them ex-Red Guards, the most likely and enthusiastic recruits anywhere to the banner of revolutionary change.

Probably a much larger number of sent-downs have found their way somewhat less dangerously back to other cities, sometimes with forged or stolen travel permits or ration cards, to crash with friends or relatives, live by their wits, or try to wangle an urban job. There have been reports in the press of street gangs composed of such refugees who live by petty theft and deal on the black market. It is hard even to guess at the numbers of such people or to estimate the size of the U-turn movement of those assigned to the countryside who make their way back to the city, but it is probably not trivial and in any case is a signal of trouble. In late 1978 and 1979 what was clearly a long pent-up reservoir of resentment and anger broke out in the rapidly changing political climate under Vice Premier Teng Hsiao-p'ing. There were massive demonstrations in Shanghai on February 5, 1979 by over a thousand middle school graduates who had been sent to the countryside during and after the Cultural Revolution. They demanded official permission to return to the city, and assignment to urban jobs. Demonstrators blocked sixty trains for twelve hours, stopped other traffic, forced their way into municipal employment offices and roughed up officials there, broke into shops and stole goods, and harangued crowds with loud hailers which they had stolen. The press reports of this outburst indicated that a similar but even larger demonstration involving over 3,000 such malcontents had rioted for several days in Shanghai in mid-December of 1978, demanding work and ration cards.[44]

The press was of course strongly critical, suggesting that although people had a right to demonstrate (?) this did not mean that they could block traffic, "create trouble, infringe on other peoples' liberty, and upset normal work and public order". Such Western-style language and argument, especially the reference to hitherto unmentioned "rights" to demonstrate, were a symptom of rapid political change. A later *Chieh-fang* story on February 11 even reported that many of the demonstrators were angered that they had been reassigned to "other areas" when they "finished" (?) their labor time in the countryside rather than being returned to their original homes in Shanghai. Press editorials and letters to the editor urged that the demonstrators be punished, but there were few suggestions that they did not have a legitimate grievance. The wind had begun to blow away from earlier revolutionary visions, even if order had to be preserved, as subsequent official statements made clear. Within a week of official pronouncements that disorder would not be tolerated, and that "irresponsible elements" would be punished and suppressed, the official New China News Agency also reported on February 23, 1979, that "98 per cent of the former capitalist businessmen and industrialists in Tientsin who were persecuted by Lin Piao and the Gang of Four have had their confiscated belongings wholly or partially given back. . . . Their bank deposits are also being unfrozen and interest on those deposits is being paid". Tientsin has also re-conferred professional titles on 95 former businessmen and industrialists and has "arranged for over 500 experienced people to take up management posts in enterprises and shops", with salaries restored, plus back pay. How better to signal that there is after all a place in China for personal ambition, and for bourgeois-style elitism?

We have seen very few glimpses for many years of the Chinese underground in any form, although underground political jokes, stories and literature have existed all along and include, among other things officially forbidden, thriller-type mystery stories (considered frivolous) and even pornography (Communist Chinese norms are highly puritanical). Now it would seem that dissident stirrings are at least a little closer to the surface, as in a two-page duplicated broadsheet distributed to foreign journalists in Peking on April 22, 1979 which protested against the "tyranny of the Mao era" and asserted "There will definitely be no modernization without freedom of thought, opinion, and publication".[45] This is a protest against the official clamp-down in late March on all demonstrations and public opposition, but until recently no one would have dared to say such things publicly, let alone distribute them to foreign journalists. The revolutionary mass line seems to be cracking, as China seems to be opting increasingly for maximum growth at maximum speed. This means, as Teng has made clear, concentration on large-scale plants, massive imports of foreign technology, and the rapid growth of cities as the major bases of development. Perhaps, especially if and as urban birth rates continue to fall, this is the best way to absorb each new age cohort seeking urban employment. But it marks a sharp turn away from earlier revolutionary and anti-urban models. And what kinds of cities will China now have to contend with?

It seems highly likely that it is the young, the radicals and Red Guards of the Cultural Revolution years, who will be the chief pushers for "liberalization", since they are the most impatient with enforced rustication and self-sacrifice and have the most to gain—and to expect—from changes which will allow them to pursue the ambition which is natural in all young people. Those who have completed secondary school (most of whom are urban) and the few who have made it to or through a university or technical school will also press for the status and life-style which education is supposed to confer. This will doubtless also include increasing demands for "free expression" and "human rights", already being mentioned more and more frequently. "Getting ahead" has always meant for most making it in the urban scene, which is where all this ferment centers. When Teng Hsiao-p'ing visited Tokyo in February of 1979 on his way back from celebrating the beginning of Sino-American "normalization" in the United States, he is said to have been asked by officials at the Japanese Foreign Ministry if he had considered the possibility that some of the many Chinese who are now going abroad for study may decide to stay in the host country rather than returning to China. Teng is reported to have said yes, he had assumed there would be such cases but he was not worried about it. One wonders how much of such confidence was whistling in the dark. Certainly the expansion of foreign contacts, including the two-way exchange of students and scholars, but also a much less cramped picture in the Chinese media of life in other countries and a big increase in foreign goods in China, must represent to many Chinese a disturbing perspective. The attractions and rewards of Western-style modernization—and they surely are many, especially for people in a developing (poor) country—are essentially urban, and individuals are most likely to obtain them for themselves in the cities.

After many years of work-study in schools and universities, where the chief emphasis was on political study and political attitudes, there is now a qualified return to traditional Chinese zeal for learning, hard competition for grades, for success in entrance exams, and expectation of status rewards. Class background is apparently no longer a major factor in admission to university; many if not most of those selected can also now enter directly from secondary school, without a period of productive labor. Such policy changes clearly favor urban youth, since the best schools are there and since urban-based parents or relatives may also be able to "help". The new policy includes an increase in the number of technical and higher secondary schools in rural areas, which are certainly badly needed; but most ambitious young people will still strongly prefer urban universities and urban careers.

What are called "key schools" have been established at all levels from primary through university, designed to select and train the most able students. Even in the capitalist West there has long been controversy over "streaming" or "tracking" in the schools, which is now apparently practiced in all schools in China. But the "key schools" are unabashedly elitist. The great majority of their graduates are said to pass the newly rigorous university entrance examinations, which very few graduates of regular schools succeed in doing. There are also at least two kinds of middle (high) schools, "agricultural" and "regular". "Peasant origin" is still given lip-service advantage for university admission, but is said to be defined so as to include urban graduates who have spent a year in the countryside. And although the cumulative spread of education facilities, especially at the higher levels, was interrupted by the Cultural Revolution, primary schooling now appears to be almost universal and "lower middle school" (through age 14 or 15) training is said to be available for about three-quarters of the appropriate age cohorts in "most areas".[46] The great weight of educational advantage has shifted even more decidedly to the cities, which is also where new, including newly elitist, graduates will seek careers. Many Chinese, including many cadres, now freely say even to foreigners that the Cultural Revolution, and especially its destructive impact on the educational system, was an unfortunate aberration, widely regretted and even blamed by some on a senile or too easily misled Mao Tse-tung.

English language is now nearly universally studied in all post-primary schools. English lessons are broadcast on the state radio, and one can now also listen freely to Voice of America broadcasts. There is a hunger for books, of all kinds, after many years of relative famine when the few bookstores carried only the works of Mao, Lenin, Marx, and Stalin. Some selected foreign books, movies, clothes, and music are beginning to be available on a still limited basis—and only in the big cities. Even contemporary Chinese literature and art (including films) are beginning to escape a little from the lifeless straitjacket imposed on them under former Culture Czarina Chiang Ch'ing (*Jiangjing*)—Mao's wife, now in disgrace as one of the "Gang of Four". These are all urban things, part of the urban world, and the cities the main windows onto a new "modern" world which most people want.

In this newly liberalized atmosphere, the young especially will be impatient with China's still slow development and will push for the strategy which accelerates it best, namely urban concentration. Many young people now freely say that they *hate* rural assignment and try to avoid it. Some are now saying to American visitors that they would rather live in the United States than in China! The radical causes of the past are being replaced, at least for the present, by a struggle for individual advancement in an urban-centered world, as the mass line and selfless serving of the people begin to give way to a degree of individualism and "freedom". Thirty years is a long time, perhaps too long, to sustain the devotion and sacrifice evoked by revolution. All revolutions grow old, tired, and lose their youthful radical bite. China has in fact sustained the radicalness of its revolution longer than any other in modern times, since the French and American revolutions of the

late eighteenth century. The deaths of Chou (*Zhou Enlai*) and
Mao in 1976 now seem to have marked the end of an era in a
much wider sense than the passing from the stage of two great
men. One must also allow a good deal for the fact that the new
generation of Chinese know only their elders' stories of the glori-
ous days in Yenan (*Yanan*), the Long March, and the early years
of the Peoples' Republic. To some the stories may now seem a
little like stirring accounts of Valley Forge which fail to stir many
American young people. Young Chinese may well find more excitement now in learning something about the rest of the world,
from which they have been cut off for so long. The rest of the
world is in fact very different from China. Some of those differences are bound to be upsetting and disruptive to the revolutionary ethic under which China has at least nominally lived for
more than a generation.

But one must not exaggerate what has happened so far, dra-
matic as it seems to read of American hotel chains being built in
China or disco dives operating in Peking. Nor should one project
such changes into the indefinite future, still less conclude that
China will soon be just like the rest of the world. There is still a
powerful revolutionary hold on the Chinese mind which is by no
means dead. France can never again be what it was before 1789,
even though Robespierre was overthrown, nor can Russia return
to its reactionary past despite the victory of Stalinism over the
revolutionary legacy of Lenin and Trotsky (not to mention
Marx). China, and most Chinese, are still concerned with social
justice, and with the human rather than merely economic consequences of growth. Both concerns are almost certainly stronger in
China than in any other country. China will long remain a dominantly peasant and rural country, and its development policies
are bound to reflect that basic circumstance. The anti-urban legacy has certainly lost some of its force and indeed seems for the
present to be almost in eclipse, but its roots are old and deep and
it seems certain to surface again, in a variety of forms, even as
cities continue to grow and to breed new elites.

Radical policies of all sorts have had strong support and determined official advocates at many periods during the past thirty

years, and China still sees itself, proudly, as a revolutionary society, *the* revolutionary model for the rest of the world. Radical
policies and their advocates are currently in deep shadow but
they have not been and cannot be completely eradicated. Teng
Hsiao-p'ing and his "pragmatic" line have of course their strong
supporters too, but they have prevailed only after intense political struggle behind the scenes and their dominance seems unlikely to last forever without challenge or modification. Future
changes, at least in the short run, seem far more likely to reflect
the struggle between opposing lines, a see-sawing between "pragmatic" and "revolutionary" policies, than to extend the present
trends indefinitely. National pride will also continue to push the
Chinese toward policies which emphasize their distinctiveness,
their unique accomplishments, and their role as a model society
rather than toward those which cast China as a second-class fol-
lower of foreign models, a poor and late entrant into a Western-
dominated competition.

And despite the new talk, there is very little individual freedom
in China. Chinese society is almost certainly the most tightly
controlled in the world, even or especially in the cities, and the
power of the Chinese state is unparalleled. As policy shifts take
place at the top, as they seem certain to do over time, they will be
carried out, whatever the messages posted on the so-called "Democracy Wall" in Peking. At the same time, policy will be affected to some extent, and perhaps more than in the past, by increasingly vocal public opinion. No state can afford to ignore
completely the felt needs of its people, and policy must maintain
some kind of relationship with changing attitudes as well as circumstances. It is to say the least thought-provoking to read press
accounts of new cosmetic shops, fashionable hairdressing establishments, and expensive dress designers in China—all of course
in the biggest cities. But Peking and Shanghai will never become
just another Paris or London; indeed it seems probable that the
present rash of urban-bourgeois trends will stimulate at least a
mild nativist and Maoist-leaning reaction. The weight of the revolutionary tradition, and Chinese pride in it, plus the pressures of
political radicals, are in combination just too strong to be swept

away so easily or so quickly. But the long-term trend does seem to be against such forces and in favor of the urban-bourgeois mode, contrary to the original revolutionary goal of a peasant-based society which would eliminate the differences between city and countryside.

There is simply no way to reproduce in the countryside, or on a rural commune, the excitement and variety of urban life, nor the amenities and diversions represented by department stores, street crowds, museums, movie houses, or sports events. Visiting film or dance-drama teams cannot do it, any more than the bare-foot doctor or commune hospital can duplicate medical services available in the cities. Material living standards, wages, and education are all on a higher level in virtually all Chinese cities than in rural areas—highest of all in the largest—and it is in the cities that the most desirable jobs will continue to be found, not only in terms of pay rates but in terms of the attendant attractions of power, responsibility, creativity, leadership, or simply elite status. And the irony of economic growth, centered in cities, is that it becomes addictive, as the Western and Japanese (and Taiwanese!) experiences demonstrate. More goods and services simply feed more appetite, producing what is aptly labelled "consumerism". The disease cannot be limited to the young, and it is already present in Chinese cities. It is perhaps the stage which follows what used to be denounced as "economism" (creeping capitalism?) with its selfish concentration on personal material gain—wages and purchasing power—instead of on the selfless serving of the people, one of the targets of the Cultural Revolution. Economism is no longer spoken about, but nascent consumerism is already visible in the competition for radios, TV sets, cameras, wrist watches, and a variety of other non-essential or even luxury goods.

Keeping up with the Joneses (Wangs) is a universal human frailty. Department stores in the big cities display a wide variety of consumer goods, many of them far from utilitarian; one hears complaints that the prices are set too high, in relation to wage levels, and that the supply is inadequate. As long as every household does not have all these and other things, including the flowered prints, fancy clothing, toys, furniture (including garden furniture!), and knick-knacks already displayed in the stores, there will be a sense of relative deprivation—and continuing pressure to keep up with the Wangs. Wage and salary rates are of course used as incentives, increasingly the dominant incentives, and they are far from equal, even in given cities. The range from lowest to highest may be as great as one to ten, and has been approximately of that order for many years.[47] But if material incentives are allowed to be important, it is difficult to prevent the rise of both "economism" and consumerism. What is now still in its early stages in China is really different only in degree from what the Chinese used to refer to scathingly as the obsession of capitalist societies with materialist bourgeois values and behavior. Desire to improve one's material lot is common to nearly all people in all societies. Truly dedicated revolutionaries and those who sought austerity were probably never more than a small minority. Now it would seem that a new wave is washing over their supposedly inspiring model as China enters a new slippery slope, as its productivity continues to rise, linked with the growth of cities. The new elites produced by development cannot be expected to conform indefinitely to revolutionary ideals or to blueprints for austerity and mass egalitarianism. How much of China's revolutionary vision, how much of its design for a better road to development, will remain?

7. China's Development Effort in Comparative Context

IT IS THIRTY YEARS SINCE THE VICTORY OF THE REVOLUTION IN China. How different has China's development pattern been, as a result of its revolutionary ideology, from what has been happening in other developing countries? How successful has it been in achieving the twin goals of rapid economic growth and of diffusion of development to all of its areas and people, by comparison with what has been accomplished in these terms elsewhere? By far the most appropriate comparison is with India, not so much because it is Asian as because in size, population, existing economic level and spatial patterns of urban-industrial development as of 1949; its balance between urban and rural, agricultural and industrial; its modern experience with colonialism and imperialism; and traditional rural-centered values, India closely parallels most aspects of China's situation. India since winning independence in 1947 has however followed a different road to development under a very different political system and thus provides a particularly useful basis for comparison, perhaps even a test or check on the effectiveness of the distinctive Chinese strategies. This chapter will therefore concentrate on a comparative analysis of the Indian and Chinese development experiences and the urban-rural balance since 1949, using comparative perspectives from other countries as appropriate. India and China are however both representative of the developing world as a whole, although they are by far the two largest samples. Both are poor, both dominantly peasant-agricultural. Foreign investment in both was largely responsible for the growth of a few big industrial cities on the coastal edge of each country (Madras, Bombay, and Calcutta were all founded by the British and by 1947 were the three biggest Indian cities—see the map on page 119). About 20 percent of the population of both countries now lives in cities. The development problems faced by both are closely similar.

The chief difficulty of almost any India-China comparisons is the great disparity in data availability. Shortage of data hampers almost all study of contemporary China, and it is only now beginning to be possible to conduct field research or even observation there beyond the briefest and most superficial level. Most observations are still limited to certain areas on carefully managed "tours" usually run by government "guides". In India, by contrast, observers may go almost anywhere, and stay as long as they please; officials and others answer questions freely; there is vigorous public discussion of virtually everything, including all aspects of government policy; and the press is as free as anywhere in the world and is highly developed. Equally important, the Census of India and a great variety of other statistical sources offer extensive and reasonably accurate data on most aspects of the country and its people and economy. There is also an immense literature, most of it in English, reporting on and analyzing every aspect of Indian development, from every conceivable point of view, by both Indians and foreigners. India is in fact a much-studied country, partly because of the very large number of active Indian intellectuals and highly trained professionals, partly because of its openness and its excellent data base, and partly because it is, after China, the largest single test case of a poor country in the process of development. India exemplifies the greatest global problem of our times and has attracted attention accordingly. China is by comparison still largely closed, lacks even an elementary data base, and although its development ef-

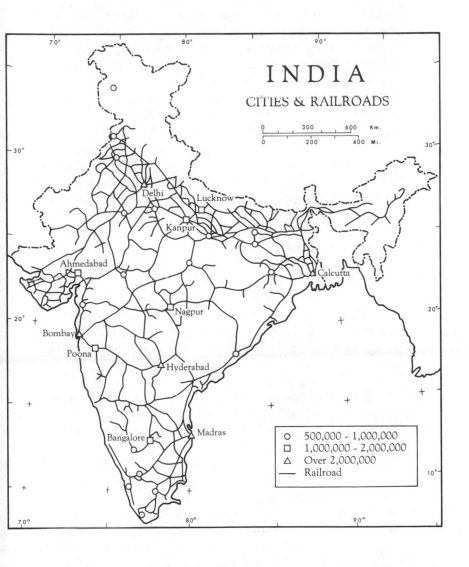

INDIA
CITIES & RAILROADS

Km.

Mi.

○	500,000 - 1,000,000
□	1,000,000 - 2,000,000
△	Over 2,000,000
—	Railroad

Delhi

Lucknow

Kanpur

Ahmedabad

Calcutta

Nagpur

Bombay

Poona

Hyderabad

Bangalore

Madras

forts have attracted much attention, much less is known in any detail about what has been accomplished.

There have however been several attempts, by Indian and Western scholars, to compare Chinese and Indian achievements quantitatively on a national basis.[48] That in itself may of course be misleading, especially when one is dealing with such large countries, both of which include a very wide range of regional variation. Unfortunately the Chinese data, such as they are, make it difficult to obtain a more accurate picture, but a national comparison is still of some usefulness and is in any case the scale on which success is usually measured. The most careful efforts so far to measure development in the two countries, following conventional techniques of economics and national income analysis, lead to what may seem to some a surprising conclusion: China and India have been just about equally successful, up to about 1976, in generating economic growth. China has been marginally ahead in the rate of industrial growth, but this is in part because the industrial base there was considerably smaller in 1949 than its equivalent in India: it is easier to double or triple a smaller output than a larger one. India has been marginally ahead in the growth of agricultural output. At least some of China's apparently slightly slower progress agriculturally (though it must be stressed that we have especially poor agricultural data from China and hence cannot be certain of anything) may be due to the mistakes and set backs of the Great Leap and the delay in the decision to divert more capital investment to the agricultural sector.[49] But whatever the statistical uncertainties, the general picture seems reasonably clear: despite the very different strategies of the two countries (and the very different images most outsiders have of each), there seems to be little difference in the results. Without any doubt, the most important reason is that both countries confront basically the same kinds and degrees of problems, as already indicated above, and that the process of economic development is long, slow, and difficult: there are no short cuts, and no cost-free solutions. Nor can ideology and slogans substitute for investment, resolve the resistant problems which all development everywhere must face, or create a magic formula for performance.

This is so despite the existence in China of a uniquely powerful central government with virtually total control over the allocation and manipulation of resources and population and with all development centrally planned. The central government in India is far weaker, hemmed in by constitutional safeguards plus provisions for a considerable degree of autonomy in the separate states (provinces) of the Indian Union, organized on a federal pattern as in the United States. There is a central planning agency, but there is also a large private sector, which is wholly dominant in agriculture and operates about half of the industrial plant. There is unrestricted labor mobility, and while there are some controls on industrial and other investment, especially where it may involve the use of scarce materials or services (including foreign exchange), the private sector operates to a large extent on a commercial market basis. Altogether, India has what might be called a "capitalist-mixed" system, not terribly different from the economic system (in these terms) in Europe, Britain, or even the United States. India has often had the image abroad of failure, of famine, hopeless poverty, and lack of development, while China's image has more often been one of success, enthusiasm, and progress. Neither image is accurate.

India has in some sense been its own worst enemy in this respect, with a free press and a very active intellectual group which continually criticize the undoubted shortcomings and problems of India's development; and it is the problems which also attract most outside attention. India is wide open to observation, investigation, and comment; and stories about the slums of Calcutta or flood refugees in Bihar make more sensational copy than more careful accounts of the slow improvement in the standard of living for most people, which is also true. For example, there have been extremely few famine deaths since well before independence, and food shortages in a few bad years (now probably a thing of the past) have almost certainly been no worse, if as bad, as Chinese food shortages in the post-Leap years and periodically since in some areas. The Chinese have been far more successful propagandists, both towards their own people and especially towards outsiders. They present a gleaming, problem-free picture of smiling, rosy-cheeked peasants harvesting what are always referred to as "bumper crops", completing new dams and power lines, and exceeding production quotas or completing new steel mills ahead of schedule. The Chinese excel at slogans and public relations, but the full reality behind the glossy magazines and official statements is impossible to discover or to see for one's self. Only through occasional accounts in the Chinese press, by reading between the lines, and by interviewing refugees can one guess at the problems and shortcomings—enough perhaps to conclude that they are about the same, and maybe of the same magnitude, as in India or any other developing country: overloaded transport systems, overcrowded cities, inadequate housing, consumer goods, and basic services; a widening urban-rural gap; and an overall growth rate, especially in agriculture, still only precariously ahead of population increases. But there is a pronounced tendency on the part of many outsiders to think positively, even admiringly, about China, and negatively and pessimistically about India. Judging especially from American reactions, it would seem that democratic systems are out of style and that what glitters is "revolution".

It would appear however that the Chinese have been more successful than the Indians, or than most other countries, in reducing the gap between the very rich and the very poor (as already discussed), and also, perhaps, in distributing the benefits of growth more adequately to all regions of the country and to rural areas. There too we cannot measure accurately for China, and it is possible that the information we have is misleading. Both China and India have made conscious decisions to accept a somewhat slower overall growth rate, at least in the short run, by diverting some of their investment in development to rural and inland areas rather than concentrating it all in the existing large cities at lower cost. As already suggested, this has been only a qualified success so far in China: most small-scale rural industry does not seem to be permanently viable and represents only a tiny proportion of the rural scene. Rural industrial development in India may in fact be as great or even greater. Urban-based dispersal has gone reasonably far in China, but has taken place in India too, and probably to about the same degree, with new or rapidly growing urban-industrial bases in nearly all the Indian states and growth also at intermediate levels. The Indians have been less successful in limiting the growth of their largest cities, which have mushroomed out of control and present serious problems of overcrowding, unemployment, and dangerous shortages of housing and basic services. But the human costs of the Chinese controls on population movement and assignment are heavy and cannot really be translated into economic terms.

Perhaps the greatest Chinese success story is in the field of public health, where a determined effort has been made to bring at least minimum health care to most of the population in most areas, through the "barefoot doctor" system of itinerant and partly-trained health workers and through a hierarchy of local clinics and commune hospitals linked to larger urban, provincial, and national centers. There are severe data problems here too, and a very wide range of health facilities, from area to area, province to province, and city to city: some remoter areas are still most inadequately covered, and there is no question of the very wide gap in medical services between the cities, especially the largest ones, and the countryside. There are no reliable data from China, even on a national basis, about mortality or morbidity rates and only fragmentary and unsatisfactory data on other aspects of health, including diet, nutritional levels, and degrees of health care. What statistics we have however suggest that by about 1960 China had passed India (which in 1950 was ahead) in hospital beds per thousand people (0.9 as against 0.61 for India), although it is less clear what has happened since 1960 in these terms. In general, it seems that the Chinese have indeed done a good job with basic public health, and perhaps marginally better than India. In India too, however, there has been a very rapid expansion of village and small town clinics and hospitals, a rising level of medical care generally, and an end to the formerly destructive inroads of the major epidemic and contagious diseases.

Perhaps the best measure of public health as well as material welfare is the sharply increasing life expectancy in India from 27 at independence to 48 in the 1971 census to approximately 54 in 1980 (there are no reliable life expectancy figures from China for comparison).[50] In well over half of the Indian states paramedical workers visit most villages regularly, as in China, and there is a reasonably effective referral system to clinics and hospitals at higher levels, assisted in India by a transport system which is much better developed, especially in rural areas, than in China. There are wide regional differences in health care facilities in both countries, but it is certainly possible that on a national average Indian rural areas, and perhaps the cities, are as well served as in China. The Chinese achievement, though rightly praised, is not unique. However, one should perhaps add that the observable improvement in rural and urban health levels, striking in both countries, is probably due primarily to improved nutrition (and sanitation plus water supply) rather than to medical intervention.

It is far more difficult to guess at overall levels of economic welfare in China in either urban or rural areas, except that the Chinese themselves acknowledge a great deal of regional disparity, and admit to income levels (perhaps also standards of living?) in the cities which are at least twice the rural average. In these gross terms, the picture in India is roughly similar. Field observation would be enormously helpful to obtain a more detailed and a more accurate impression, but that is still not possible in China except on the most hurried and superficial basis. Nevertheless, even in the two or three weeks of highly managed tourism which is all most outsiders can obtain, it is possible to see some things and to increase somewhat the basis for comparison. Most people in China, urban and rural, look adequately nourished, adequately clothed, and free of disease—in all these respects an enormous change from the 1940's. It has been a massive achievement to have provided these basic essentials for a population which has nearly doubled since then, and to yield probably some net improvement per capita. Housing and other goods and services are still scarce, judging from what most people seem to own or to have in their houses, what is available in shops, prices, and rationing. But most people seem healthy and cheerful; most villages, towns, and cities clean and well-organized—on such an impressionistic basis, more so than, for example, in the Middle East or most of Latin America.

India is observable for far longer periods of stay and with few limits on the observer.[51] There too, especially in the villages which are necessarily the heart of the development problem for both countries, there is a generally well-nourished, well-clothed, and healthy population now (as opposed to the 1940's or even 1950's), with little or no indication of disease or malnutrition even in the poorest areas (e.g., Bihar, Madhya Pradesh, Kerala) which in China are usually closed to foreign visitors, who see only what the Chinese want them to see. One of the changes in India since the 1950's which seems especially striking is the very large number of chickens, ducks, and *pigs*, in addition to sheep, goats, and cattle, in most rural areas, a change which has a lot to do with improved levels of nutrition. Village children, often the first to show the signs of malnutrition and disease, seem in excellent shape nearly everywhere. Paved roads and regular bus services now reach every village in India (as of the end of 1979), and there are clouds of bicycles in every rural area (as well as in the cities), many times the numbers in China. Electric power seems more widely available in villages and rural areas than in China, and power-driven pumps plus large new dams provide new amounts of irrigation almost everywhere. New irrigation (more than doubled even since 1968); greatly increased fertilizer production (more than quadrupled since 1968); and new high-yielding varieties of wheat and rice (the "Green Revolution") are of course responsible for India's good overall record in agriculture. Even village dogs, formerly miserable specimens, now look well fed and healthy! Nearly every town and many villages now have a medical clinic and/or a visiting health worker, but the new ease of movement—by bicycle, bus and train—may make it less necessary to establish medical facilities in rural areas as opposed to bringing patients in to better equipped urban centers.

The range of goods in village and small town shops (as well as in cities) is very much greater than in China, and includes many of foreign origin; and prices are lower in relation to real income. (Wages and income distribution patterns are relatively easily determined for India and for China with at least reasonable approximation.) There is no rationing. Housing is inadequate and often miserable and dilapidated, but the Indian climate may make that less of a hardship than it might otherwise be, and housing quality seems very roughly comparable to China's. Indian villages and cities are far dirtier and infinitely more fly-ridden than Chinese, but in general one is struck by the air of exuberant vitality and well-being in rural India as compared with twenty or thirty years ago. There are of course sharp regional variations, but almost nowhere does one see real misery in rural India (except of course on an individual basis), and there is a widespread cheerfulness and sense of fun which accord poorly with images of fatalistic or hopeless poverty. What has been called the Little Tradition, with its frequent festivals, ceremonies, and simple amusements may be preserved more vigorously in rural India than anywhere, and certainly more so than in revolutionary China, where the state tries to suppress it. In village and small town India it adds a dimension of enjoyment beyond the limits of hard work (which is the lot of peasants everywhere) that is largely lacking in China. It shows in people's behavior. In any case, one senses a healthy and vibrant quality in rural India, and a material base which has improved greatly in the past two or three decades. Such an impressionistic picture may of course be misleading, however real, but in those terms it seems to fit the image which the Chinese seek to give of *their* rural areas and people— and perhaps to fit it better. Rural India still must confront massive development problems, and the fight against poverty is far from being over. But it would appear that there, as in China, the basic battle for survival has been won and an important corner turned, toward a more or less securely, if slowly, rising standard of living, at least for most people.

It is in India's cities that one does see large-scale misery, and dismaying squalor. There one can sense the despair of masses of urban unemployed, many of them beggars, many of them diseased, living and sleeping on the streets or in wretched squatter shacks (which Chinese controls have largely cleaned out) or crowded together in what used to be called tenements in the West, without piped water, schools, adequate diet or medical care, and often without prospects of improvement. One cannot say without hope, because it is hope which has brought most of them to the cities. There too one senses a kind of vitality which often seems lacking in Chinese cities; even for the worst slums there are the endless excitements of a bustling city around them, more colorful for all its squalor than the seemingly dreary human and cultural landscape of towns and cities in the Peoples' Republic where controls, rationing, hard work, and general austerity leave little scope for variety. Indian cities pulsate with life virtually around the clock. Foreigners complain that Chinese cities are dead after dark, thus betraying their bourgeois values. Indian cities also contain a large proportion of middle class people and professionals, and a few rich, some of them enormously so, which sharpens the contrast with the masses of poor. Such imbalances, and the uncontrolled growth, overcrowding, and miserable conditions of life for so many in the largest cities, seem to cry out for correction. Perhaps the Chinese way is better. . . .

Another difference needs to be noted, one which may have an important bearing on development. China until recently purposely restricted the growth of middle schools (high schools), and especially of universities, in favor of the work-study system, agricultural middle schools, technical institutes, and on-the-job training programs.[52] This resulted in part from the problems of allocating scarce funds—education is expensive—and in part from mistrust of intellectuals and potential elites. Education at all levels has stressed immediately practical work skills and work experience, with little attention allowed for research or for more general education. (As already pointed out, this ran counter to the long Chinese tradition of respect for learning, and was very unpopular with many Chinese, especially the young, for obvious reasons.) Many have questioned the wisdom of such a policy in view of the need to train research scientists and to maintain or augment a structure, and a scale, of education which can also produce scholars, teachers, managers, planners, and administrators as well as simple technicians. All are necessary for development, and especially for its perhaps equally important non-economic aspects. China still has an acute shortage of scientists, research scholars, high-level technicians, and other professionals, which has almost certainly hampered as well as warped its development in important ways; it is not enough merely to "learn from the peasants and workers".[53]

In India by contrast there has been a rapid expansion of high schools and universities, as well as technical training institutes. The price this exacts, apart from the costs of the education, is the army of unemployed or mis-employed graduates and intellectuals, most of them in the cities, for whom the system is not growing rapidly enough to provide suitable room. That too is a tragic waste and a serious problem. But the Indian educational system, for all its undoubted faults, has produced a huge number of trained professionals in almost every field, as well trained and competent as any in the world, and probably far more proportionately than in any developing country. This resource is not as fully used as it should be; its effectiveness is blunted by bureaucratism, over-specialization, and the reluctance of many professionals to serve in the rural areas where they are most needed; but it has certainly helped to maintain or accelerate economic growth. The Indian pool of highly sophisticated and cosmopolitan academics, scientists, economists, planners, journalists, administrators, technicians, managers, and entrepreneurs contrasts sharply with the acute shortage of such people in China; it enhances the impression that at least the leading edge of India is the reverse of backward, a leading edge which can be critically important. In China, while the gap between wealthy urban sophisticates at the top and beggars at the bottom is absent, or at least far less noticeable, Chinese knowledge of the rest of the world and China's pool of people competent to cope with the scientific and technical tasks of modern-style development is seriously limited, in a way which clearly has impeded economic growth. China has been largely closed to the outside world, India wide open, and the results show.

In the critical matter of transport, India has had a further advantage in inheriting from the colonial period a well-developed national railroad, and telecommunications network. China's railroad system began to develop much later and was still in its early stages (except for Japanese-controlled Manchuria) in 1949, while road development was negligible. Many new lines have been built, new roads constructed, and rolling stock and trucks produced, but China is an immense country and the transport gap cannot be filled so quickly. Railway and road building are terribly expensive and demand chronically scarce materials: steel and cement. Transport is only a means to an end, albeit an essential one; it cannot be eaten or worn or used to make things. The need for especially heavy and continuing investments in transport in China thus represents a drain of scarce investment, which has been proportionately less burdensome in India. Transport is inadequate to demand in India too, as in all developing countries, where transport shortages are usually the chief bottleneck. In a way, this is a sign that economic growth is taking place, putting more and more demands on the transport system and outrunning its ability to keep pace. But the problem is certainly more severe in China, and the transport system even less able to keep up.

As one indication of India's lead in this respect (and perhaps also of different planning decisions), Indian railways are increasingly electrified, including many long-distance and high-speed lines; the rest is diesel, and steam locomotives are almost entirely gone. In the Chinese railway system coal-burning locomotives are still dominant and are still being built in large numbers, taking advantage of China's huge reserves of coal, but at considerable loss in efficiency. Dieselization is increasing, especially as China's new oil reserves come into larger production, but one of the pleasures for foreigners of a trip to China is still the chance to ride behind a *real* steam locomotive, flags flying and brass shining. Trucks and other road vehicles, as well as miles of paved highway, are also still grossly inadequate in China, and in both respects India (which like China manufactures almost all its own railway equipment and vehicles) is far ahead in *per capita* terms, and continues to improve its network: total railway and road haulage doubled from 1950 to 1970, and nearly tripled the 1950 figure in 1979 (comparable figures from China are, needless to say, not available). This in itself tends to favor urban concentration, as everywhere, and as it seems certain to do also in China as transport there improves. The Chinese emphasis until recently on rural industry, local self-reliance, and dispersal resulted importantly from transport shortages as well as from ideological goals.

India too has a longstanding anti-urban tradition, and an anti-urban pro-rural legacy which still influences policy. It derives from the same anti-imperialist roots as in China, since most of India's modern-style urban growth took place under colonial control during the British period. It was primarily anti-colonial feelings which prompted the Gandhian ideological response, with its emphasis on the village as the best preserver and vehicle of an *Indian* way of life, and its opposition to Western-style industrial cities with their soul-destroying qualities and their supposedly parasitic exploitation of the countryside.

> If the village perishes, India will perish too. Therefore we have to concentrate on the village being self-contained, manufacturing mainly for use. Provided the character of village industry is maintained, there would be no objection to villagers using even the modern machines and tools that they can make and can afford to use[54]. . . .
> Cities would take their natural place and not appear as unnatural, congested spots or boils on the body-politic as they are today. . . . If the hearts of the city-dwellers remain rooted in the villages, if they become village-minded, all other things will automatically follow, and the boil will quickly heal.[55]

The parallel with Chinese Communist ideas about village and city is striking.[56] Gandhi (and many of his contemporary followers) speak as if they believed it might be possible somehow to select from the package of industrialization only those things which are desirable and which could be accomplished without large urban concentrations and their consequences, presumably being produced instead in small rural units and in some happy combination with traditional methods and village values. It is understandable that the Gandhian ideal has remained for the most part—perhaps like the Maoist ideal—just that: a useful nationalist rallying ground, an inspiring vision which made people feel good, but not a practical plan for development. The urgency of development is too great to permit much more than symbolic attention to the Gandhian—or the Maoist—vision. Even Nehru felt obliged to disavow Gandhi's anti-industrialism. He and successive leaders and planners have had to pursue industrial growth as fast and as efficiently as possible, which means primarily in large cities, including those over-crowded dark Satanic mills inherited from colonialism.

Nevertheless, the Gandhian ideal is still powerful, and Indian planning has tried, about as hard and with about as much success as in China, to tilt the balance of investment and development at least to some degree toward the rural areas. It has also recognized, although somewhat belatedly, and partly in response to earlier Chinese efforts, that rural development cannot be created from the top down or from outside nearly as effectively as from a grass-roots approach which involves rural people themselves as participants rather than merely as passive recipients of resented and mistrusted outside directives. Indian planning recognizes that to divert scarce capital and resources from lower-cost and faster nuclei of growth in large cities to support rural or smaller-scale development will make overall growth slower and more expensive, something which no poor country can contemplate easily. The question is one of the acceptable balance, precisely as in China, when strong ideological and non-economic goals contend with the imperatives of growth *per se*. As in China, or in any system, these are political decisions; as such, they reflect a varying political climate.

The election of the Janata government in 1977 led by Morarji Desai, an avowed Gandhian, marked a political change in India which further tipped the balance toward rural development. There are expanded programs for low-interest loans and subsidies to rural industries, for the Small Farmers Development

Agency, for so-called "backward" and "tribal" areas, for "drought-prone areas," and for local district planning. All of these programs had been in existence for many years, but under Desai were further pushed. Small-scale industries are served by 16 Institutes, 55 Extension Centers, and a great number of training and research centers, model projects, mobile vans, prototype equipment, and local demonstrations. The central government reserves 15 per cent of scarce materials, domestic and imported, for small-scale industry. Long before the Janata government such efforts had produced results; the production of hand-woven cloth (khaddi), the most important single rural industry, increased over four times between 1955 and 1971, and there were equivalent increases in small-scale rural processing of agricultural goods, and the production of leather, matches, sugar, soap, paper, pottery, artisan goods, and other such items. These trends have accelerated since 1977, and there is promising new research on the adaptation of solar and organic (mainly dung) energy sources for village use, plus the development of "polyester khaddi" which uses machine-made synthetic yarn to produce a high-quality cloth at low cost. More effort and capital have also been put into building rural hospitals, clinics, roads, and bus routes, a change quickly evident.[57] It is perhaps ironic that as India appears to have increased its tilt toward small-scale and indigenous rural development and probably now has proportionately more of its total industrial output coming from small-scale rural producers, China under Hua Kuo-feng (*Hua Guofeng*) and Teng Hsiaop'ing appears to be moving in the opposite direction, in favor of large urban plants and imported technology, and with an educational system now concentrated more on the production of highly trained specialists. We cannot measure either balance accurately (even in India the data on small-scale industry are ambiguous—perhaps understandably given its nature—and in particular do not distinguish adequately between urban and rural), but it would seem that what once appeared to be somewhat divergent strategies are now moving toward convergence. The difference remains that central planning in India is far less powerful than in China. The Indian private sector will continue to concentrate its investment in the big cities—and the state will continue to be tempted, for the most part successfully, to do the same, since industrial growth will remain cheaper and faster there, while reserving only a relatively small part for rural development. The planned investment by the central government in a few large-scale plants purposely located in "backward" rural areas, such as the big steel plants at Bhilai in Madhya Pradesh or at Rourkela in Orissa, have had disappointing results in stimulating other forms of local growth as was hoped. They have remained largely "enclave economies", with few effective linkages with even the immediately surrounding areas—and they still produce at higher cost than better located plants. Even the Janata government could not change that, as in India's democratic framework government generally can do little even if it tries to control the further growth of the large cities or to move more than a small amount of industrialization to the countryside.

The same is true for the Indian planners' continued emphasis on the need for filling out a better balanced urban hierarchy. Cities over 100,000 are still increasing most rapidly, and already contain well over half of the total urban population. The number of villages also continues to increase, and their inhabitants hold steady at about 80 per cent of total population. In between, the smaller and intermediate towns and cities grow much less rapidly and hold a declining proportion of India's people even as their absolute numbers rise. The polarization process which the planners criticize and which is one of the biggest problems of development everywhere seems if anything to be increasing. The reasons are of course economic, and they are essentially beyond the planners' powers to alter. Planning cannot really create a balanced urban hierarchy, except by forced re-settlement. In India, it is encouraging to find a vigorous growth of small and intermediate towns and cities in Punjab and Tamilnadu—but in direct, and causal, relationship to regional economic development rather than in response to planning efforts. In the less developed states and regions, polarization continues and urban-rural linkages are weak, to the detriment of the rural areas. It is discouraging, but it is hardly surprising, since this is the nature of the development process everywhere. The early stages of all economic development experiences have seen an increase rather than a narrowing of the urban-rural gap, as is also still clearly happening in China. It takes time, and a high level of development, for growth and its benefits to trickle down from the cities. But, eventually, that does happen, as it has in all of the "developed" countries.

As change takes place, it is impossible to preserve the traditional character of the village. That is no doubt regrettable in many respects, but it is the price which must be paid for a better material life for most people. Nor can the village, however injected with "modernization", let alone preserved in its traditional form, be counted on to produce anti-biotics, steel and cement for hospitals, X-ray equipment, tractors, and generators, except perhaps in token amounts, at high cost, and as part of a primarily city-based technological system. Any form of growth means and requires change, disruption, erosion of traditional culture, and, at least in the short run, relative suffering or deprivation for many—including of course the urban poor. The early stages of development have always included many unlovely features. Meanwhile many of the small and intermediate towns and cities which theoretically are so desirable to fill out the hierarchy of diffusion and build better urban-rural linkages are often pretty dreadful places, lacking the traditional charms of the village but lacking also many of the amenities, variety, opportunities, and excitements of the big cities. Why should people flock there, especially in India where movement is relatively free, and easier all the time, when they can almost as easily go to the larger cities where at least there is the hope of something worth having? Industry also finds little advantage in locating in small or intermediate as opposed to larger places (which of course have grown large precisely for that reason), and hence employment is also concentrated there.

There is nothing "wrong" about any of this, however regrettable it may be; it is the natural process of development, which should now be familiar, including the problems, imbalances, faults, and human losses of its early stages. Eventually the smaller and intermediate towns and cities may become like their counterparts in Europe, Japan, or North America, now in many ways pleasanter places to live than the big cities but in any case equally well provided with both essentials like good roads, housing, schools, hospitals, and basic services and with many amenities. But it takes time—and of course all developing countries are un-derstandably impatient. It would help if they would accept these realities of growth, remember the long Western experience ear-lier, and realize that it is not India's or China's or Africa's *fault* that development is slow, produces disruptive change, destroys traditional culture, causes much human misery, and encounters seemingly endless rough spots along its path. The objective—a better life for most people—is worth it, although it may in fact be for some a better life for their grand or even great-grand children.

Chinese development strategy has emphasized a grass-roots approach and the mass line, and has been much admired as a re-sult, perhaps especially in India, where there has been much dis-illusionment with earlier top-down approaches. Government is also seen as offering mainly empty promises and as hamstrung by bureaucracy, petty corruption, and politics. One does indeed eas-ily get the impression that one of India's problems, stemming from its emphasis on education and its over-supply of trained elites, is a superfluity of status-conscious planners, managers, and bureaucrats, and too few who are willing to do real work or to take initiative, especially not at the village level. If the pun can be forgiven, there are too many chiefs and not enough indians among them. But India also has the enormous advantage of a genuine democracy with free speech and action at all levels, pub-lic discussion of all issues, and a tappable reservoir of popular pressure on virtually any matter. This also leaves room for a great variety of individual and group initiatives, and a variety of local solutions to development problems, which work as a rule far bet-ter than solutions designed or directed from Delhi. In the longer run, it is just possible that democratic initiatives of this sort may also work better than the mass line, at least in its more regimented form; it too was after all imposed from the top down and can lose its vitality and usefulness, like all slogans or formulas, when un-imaginatively applied, as it has often been. What is needed is scope for those in any society who have imagination and energy to plan and lead development, and to evoke rather than commandeer mass participation.

But whatever the longer-term fate of the Janata Party (an uneasy coalition at best), the political balance in India seems clearly to have shifted increasingly away from a virtual monopoly of power by a small elite at the center to a more-and-more organized "poor majority" based primarily in the separate states and districts. The Congress Party, once a monolithic power bloc, has lost its supra-dominant position and is now more accurately seen as a coalition of regional and local groups and interests. Political leaders at every level and in any party will necessarily have to pay increasing attention to local and regional needs—which means primarily rural development programs. It is in such a context that the election of the Janata government in 1977 can be regarded as a watershed, signalling a change which seems likely to outlast the careers of individual politicians or perhaps even existing party structures. Such a change will certainly weaken the central or federal power, but may stimulate greater local participation, greater emphasis on rural programs, and perhaps a tilting of the development balance away from the big cities.

Can or should the balance be tilted in favor of equality, between city and countryside and between different regions of China and India? Both countries are big enough to include some extreme regional variation? It is understandable that both should want to correct especially the regional imbalances created by foreign-dominated planning and investment in a few large coastal cities, and should strive to shape their independent development so as to serve the interests of each country as a whole, which means attention to previously neglected rural areas and to the needs of the peasants. But there can never be, under any economic or political system no matter how totally planned, equality of welfare, opportunity, or living conditions between city and country or between different regions. It is a point perhaps too obvious to elaborate, and yet it is so often assumed away. Regional differences are a fact of life—nor are all of such differences necessarily undesirable. Those which are, in basic material welfare especially, are of course regrettable, but to try to remove them is perhaps like trying to abolish other unpleasant facts of life like old age, sickness, or personal tragedy. Planning can and certainly should try to moderate the extremes of regional and city-country differences, as both India and China are doing, and perhaps with about equal success—far from complete in both cases. In fact, there seems little doubt that the urban-rural gap in both countries has continued to widen since 1949 as mainly urban-centered development has progressed. This is a serious problem, but it does not mean that development has failed, only that it is still in its early stages, and that something is happening.

Rural and peasant living standards in both China and India have improved substantially since 1949, although the improvement can be better measured and observed in India. Development has simply taken place faster in the cities. Perhaps the best course, as the Chinese now appear to think, is to let that universal and probably inevitable process continue. Industrialization is fastest and cheapest in urban concentrations. In the short run, this produces undesirable polarization, but in the longer run it seems likely that the full fruits of development will reach the countryside sooner and better by following a strategy which maximizes growth. Diffusion can take place far more effectively when the total industrial-technological system is larger and more sophisticated, and when that also makes it possible to construct an adequate system of transport and full mobility. All economic development involves short-run sacrifices for long-term gains. Urban concentration and consequent polarization may be the most important of these sacrifices, for most of the country and its people, in return for their own long-term gain in the form of a better life: fertilizers and irrigation equipment, hospitals, schools, housing, diet, clothing, consumer goods, and amenities. Village-level contributions to this process can be minimal at best, or even token, if development is to be rapid and cost-effective.

Even token participation may however be of great importance, as the Chinese model may demonstrate, at least in its ideal form. Shang-shan hsia-hsiang may not be permanently viable, nor any large share for small-scale rural industry, but the tapping of local initiatives and the involving of rural people as active participants in improving their own welfare can make a vital contribution. Local efforts to use local resources, human and non-human, without depending on or waiting for outside injections of capital, materials, technology, or expertise from an already straining and distant urban base make the best kind of sense, and can commit people to change through self-improvement infinitely more effectively than top-down programs or directives. Not much can happen in the short run if the rural areas merely wait for the urban sector to rescue them, and even in the longer run rural development will be retarded if it cannot be pushed and even led by rural people themselves. This is probably the chief virtue, and the chief lesson, of the Chinese model; all developing countries need to learn how to walk on two legs. The rural leg will remain shorter for a long time, but limping is a great deal better than standing still—and a lot better for morale, which is one of the critical factors in development anywhere. People need to be convinced by their own experience that a better life is possible through their own efforts. The Chinese must be given great credit, as most Indians do, for achieving a massive breakthrough in the fight against poverty through mass line mobilization for walking on two legs. The Chinese model could ideally be improved on—as perhaps the Indians can—by allowing more scope for voluntarism and for genuinely local or even individual initiative. But the idea and the formula are right, and can provide a major boost to development everywhere.

Meanwhile, both India and China, it seems, must put up with urban concentration. Indian central planning has largely lacked the power to do otherwise, and China appears to have concluded from its own experience that the most it makes sense to attempt is to limit the growth of its largest cities by locating new industry elsewhere and controlling the movement of its population. Both countries have rightly oriented their industrial structures to give priority to producing what agriculture needs: fertilizers, pumps, steel and cement for irrigation projects, pesticides, tractors and machinery, and the materials for research and development in agriculture. Some investment must also continue to be diverted from the urban-industrial sector in both countries to provide basic forms of development in rural areas: clinics, hospitals, schools, roads, even if this has the effect of slowing somewhat the rate of overall growth. But there can be no hope of closing the urban-rural gap or of evening out regional economic differences (even if that were desirable in any complete form) for a very long time, if ever. The most developed countries in the world retain wide regional economic differences, spatial pockets of relative poverty, and different worlds as between city and countryside. This is not all necessarily bad, but in any case it is beyond the powers of any human agency to completely even out such differences. In the meantime, regional and urban-rural differences seem more likely to increase than to decrease as Indian and Chinese development proceed. This is a severe blow to the ideological goals of both, and will be a continuing worry to Chinese and Indian planners. But the development imperative demands priority, and that means urban concentration. Whatever its undoubted problems and its unattractive aspects, it is the quickest and cheapest road to growth, and to a better life eventually for all Indians and Chinese. Between them they make up well over a third of the population of the world, but nearly two thirds of the developing world. India and China represent the essence of the development problem for all poor countries, and have led the way in working out solutions. More than Indian or Chinese interests hang on the outcome.

8. Some Conclusions, and the Future

IT IS DIFFICULT TO GET A CLEAR PICTURE EITHER OF WHAT CHInese economic planning intends, in any specific detail, or of what has been accomplished. Official pronouncements are highly general, and press reports usually deal with specific cases but are at best haphazard and, like the official statements, highly politicized and often vague. At the first session of the Fifth National People's Congress on February 26, 1978, Chairman Hua Kuo-feng delivered what is still the major comprehensive statement on China's plans for the post-Mao era. It is worth quoting from here (in small part only—the statement runs to nearly forty pages) both as a sample of official language and for what hints it contains of China's evolving image of its own future:

> Chairman Mao [has] summed up the history of imperialist aggression against China and our people's struggle against it over the past century. He regarded the transformation of our economic and technological backwardness as a question of life and death for the nation, bringing into sharp relief the importance and urgency of socialist construction. [This is the official phrase for economic development.] In studying

Chairman Mao's teachings afresh, we can all see more clearly than ever that the socialist modernization of our agriculture, industry, national defense, and science and technology [these are referred to as the "four modernizations"] is not merely an important economic task; it is above all an urgent political task. . . . We must race against time to strengthen ourselves economically and heighten our defense capabilities at top speed. . . . Speeding up socialist modernization . . . is likewise highly important. Only thus can we further consolidate the worker-peasant alliance. . . . Only thus can we steadily raise the level of the people's material and cultural life and gradually eliminate the distinctions between mental and manual labor. And only thus can we fully consolidate the dictatorship of the proletariat and prevent capitalist restoration. . . . We must be steadfast in grasping class struggle as the key link. . . . We must adhere to the principle "Grasp revolution, promote production and other work and preparedness against war", and simultaneously press on with the three revolutionary movements of class struggle, the struggle for production, and scientific experiment.

By the end of this century, the output of major agricultural products is expected to reach or surpass advanced world levels and the output of major industrial products to approach, equal, or outstrip that of the most developed capitalist countries. . . . Our economic and technical norms must approach, equal, or surpass advanced world levels. . . . By then China will have a new look and stand unshakably in the East as a modern, powerful, socialist country.

With the completion of an independent and fairly comprehensive industrial complex and economic system for the whole country, we shall in the main have built up a regional economic system in each of the six major regions, that is, the southwest, the northwest, the central south, the east, the north, and northeast China, and turned our interior into a powerful strategic rear base. . . . Meanwhile the state plans to build or complete 120 large-scale projects, including ten iron and steel complexes, nine non-ferrous metal complexes,

eight coal mines, ten oil and gas fields, 30 power stations, six
new trunk railways, and five key harbors. . . . This will be
decisive in changing the backward state of our basic industries. . . . Every attention must also be given to the development of medium-scale and small enterprises, [which] should
come under the plans. . . . Where they compete with the
large enterprises for supplies of raw and semi-finished materials or for fuel or power, the matter must be given overall
consideration and properly solved to ensure that the needs of
the large enterprises are fully met. . . . We should as far as
possible avoid crowding the big cities with new construction
units and should build more small and medium-sized towns
and cities. . . . There should be a big increase in foreign
trade. . . . We must resolutely combat the spendthrift style
. . . and the prodigal bourgeois style of indulgence in extrava-
gance and waste. We must foster the fine tradition of waging
hard struggles and building the country with diligence and
thrift. . . .

Great efforts must be made to increase the supply of non-
staple foodstuffs for urban consumers [i.e., presumably vegetables, meat, fish, and poultry, and fruit]. . . . Vigorous action should be taken to develop collective welfare and urban
public utilities so as to facilitate production and provide
amenities for the people. . . . The elimination of pollution
and the protection of the environment are a major issue involving the people's health, an issue to which we must attach
great importance. We must draw up regulations to protect
the environment and make sure that related problems are
satisfactorily solved. . . . We must study hard and work well
. . . thus propelling the national economy forward at high
speed. . . . We must stick to the policy of "making the past
serve the present" and "making things foreign serve China".
We must conscientiously study the advanced science and
technology of all countries and turn them to our account. . . .
We should not adopt a policy prohibiting people from coming into contact with the false, the ugly, and the hostile, . . .
for "it will lead to mental deterioration, one-track minds, and

unpreparedness to face the world and meet challenges". Our purpose in providing the people with selections of needed negative material is to fortify and immunize them . . .

Reviewing the past and looking forward into the future, we are fortified by our boundless confidence that we will win new and still greater victories in our socialist revolution and socialist construction.[58]

These are the only even partly specific references to economic or urban matters in the entire document. They do not help very much, but the effort to touch all bases, to invoke Mao's canonical approval, and to push both political-ideological and economic goals is interesting. It is indeed largely the same prescription which Mao advocated, with the difference that foreign trade and foreign technology are now accepted instead of emphasizing self-reliance. But there is the same insistence on "eliminating the distinctions between town and country", the same ambitious (probably over-ambitious) development goals, the same fine-sounding dedication to the "elimination of pollution", and the same confidence that new exposure to the outside world and the blandishments of consumerism will merely "immunize" rather than corrupt the Chinese people. More recently, in May and June of 1979, Hua announced a scaling-down of China's development goals: "Starting from 1979, we are shifting the focus of our work to a modification program" (i.e., of economic goals) "so China needs an international environment of peace in order to build up our country".[59] Full details of this reduction have not been issued, but it is possible that Teng-Hsiao-p'ing, who has been the chief promoter of all-out development and the import of foreign technology, may have encountered political trouble (not for the first time in his checkered career) by pushing for growth beyond China's realistic ability, especially to pay for massive foreign imports (which in any case represent a sensitive political issue).

It should be noted however that Hua's 1978 Report stresses the building of "120 large-scale projects" in the most basic industries, and specifically states that medium-scale and small enterprises "must come under the plans" and must yield full priority to the large-scale plants wherever there is competition for materials, fuel, or power. Urban crowding is to be avoided "as far as possible", whatever that may mean, but the emphasis on large plants clearly does mean that China has decided in favor of city-based industrialization as the fastest and most cost-effective way to growth and that the peasant-rural vision of development is to be largely abandoned, at least for the present. Regional industrial bases are to be continued and expanded, but predominantly in big cities.

There have been rather vague statements in the Chinese press (as for example in a September 27, 1978 editorial in *Jen-min Jih-pao* [People's Daily]) about plans to move (i.e., forcibly transfer) millions of peasants to "small" industrial towns of less than 100,000 population by 1985, but with no other details given. Cities of that size do appear to have been increasing rapidly in number since 1951, and especially since 1968, perhaps faster than overall urbanization, but again data shortages and uncertainties make it hard to be sure, as well as to discover precisely what sorts of industries would be located there and in what relationship to both larger and smaller enterprises in big cities and rural communes. This may suggest simply a planners' effort to "fill in the urban hierarchy", as in India, as a means of hastening the diffusion of development.

Both countries are still to a large degree molecular, composed of thousands of village-based communities where the bulk of the total population lives. The problem remains how best to make an impact on their welfare levels. Both countries have answered by concentrating investment in a few large urban centers in order to accelerate overall growth at least cost, with proportionately smaller gestures at rural-based development, trusting that in the longer run urban-based production and services will become more readily available to rural areas, through a combination of "trickle-down" and specific central planning. Meanwhile both urban and "rural" industry concentrate on production of essentials for increasing agricultural output: fertilizers, irrigation equipment, pesticides, crop research, tractors, and so on. It is all a rational formula, and almost certainly the right one for both countries, which both have come to after long years of experience, including some expensive trial and error as alternate formulas were pursued. But it involves at least a qualified turning of the back on Gandhian and Maoist visions of a village-based answer to Western-style development in industrial cities, and an unspoken willingness to follow essentially the same path to growth.

Poverty and the urgency of the need for growth impose hard choices, even on radical revolutionaries. There is also much to be said for the common stereotype that at root, whatever their revolutionary enthusiasms, Chinese are above all pragmatists, as Mao himself has demonstrated. There has been a continuing conflict in China for more than three decades between ideology and economic growth; it has been differently resolved at different times, and the present apparent resolution is unlikely to rest unchanged. But when ideology has impinged too hard on growth goals, it has quietly been set aside or modified, as after the Great Leap, after the Cultural Revolution, and after the death of Mao. Economic goals seem now to be more in the ascendant than at any time since 1949. After thirty years of revolution, China seems to have passed the peak of its radical phase, and is increasingly stressing the need to overcome its acknowledged technological backwardness and relative poverty, in keeping with its strong centuries-old national pride, further buttressed by the Maoist ethic to excel.

If we are to examine the Chinese experience with profit, it is important not to be so carried away by its ideological goals as not to see its economic realities, and the extent to which the Chinese have had to compromise their ideals. They are often more realistic about this than are many starry-eyed but inadequately informed outsiders and visitors, who are impressed by what they see, understandably enthused by the Maoist vision, and contrast these selected aspects of revolutionary China with what they know in far more representative detail about their own countries and their own cities at home. The Chinese freely acknowledge that there are still many unresolved problems, still much to learn, still poverty and technological backwardness to overcome, still the right balance of development policy to determine. And in their actions, the Chinese planners seem to have concluded that basic hard-fact conflicts will prevent anything like full realization of the most exciting aspects of the Maoist model, especially an alternative to urban-industrial concentration, the elimination of urban-rural differences, and the transformation of the nature of cities.

The former treaty ports are still by far the largest cities and industrial bases, after more than thirty years of planning supposedly dedicated to quite different goals. Genuinely small-scale and rural industry employs at most 3 per cent of the rural labor force, and accounts for probably something less than 10 per cent of total industrial production, a proportion which seems likely to continue falling after a peak in the early 1970's. Cities over 100,000 appear to continue to grow faster than small towns. There were only nine cities at the time of the 1953 census with populations over one million; in 1980, there appear to be about 24, most of them former treaty ports. Shanghai remains by a large margin the country's biggest city—and politically its most troublesome, as could easily have been predicted.

With all of this urban growth, it has been impossible to prevent the consequent growth of new urban elites, and the disturbing beginnings of urban consumerism. It is in the cities that the most desirable and highest status jobs will continue to be found—even in Ta Ch'ing—and the attractions of higher pay, power, responsibility, creativity, and leadership. Nor is it possible to transfer to the countryside the excitement and variety of urban life, including the diversions and amenities represented by large well-stocked department and other stores, street crowds, museums, universities, movie houses and theatres, sports events, parks, and the indefinable glitter of almost any city, even in a Maoist China where standards are utilitarian and puritanical, not to say drab. Education, health care, probably diet, and possibly even housing (for some) are also all at a higher standard in the cities than in the rural areas. The cities have their problems, and urban life is far from easy, affluent, or gracious for almost anyone. Crowding is excessive, housing and basic services seriously inadequate, and work is hard, long, and often tedious. But it is a different world from that of the countryside, and one which the majority of Chinese, despite the Maoist vision, seem to prefer and even to run risks to enter. Urban-rural differences have almost certainly increased since 1949, whatever the Maoist goals. This has been and remains one of the prices of development. China will have to settle for reducing some of the sharper edges of the differences, for example by expanding rural medical care and education facilities. But rural communes will never have even the Chinese equivalent of a big city department store branch, and all that implies. The Bergdorf-Goodman world will stay—and will thrive—in Shanghai and Peking.

Galloping urban consumerism may be China's number one problem in the coming years. As suggested earlier, there are signs that it has already begun, and that "bourgeois values", never perhaps very far below the surface especially in Shanghai, have begun to break out in the competition for television sets, "frivolous" clothing, literature, art, music, even hair styling, and a craze particularly among the young for almost anything Western. One of the ironies of economic development is that it becomes addictive. As productivity rises and technological improvement progresses, pressures build up for more and better consumer goods, a process which can only be accelerated by China's now widening contacts with the rest of the world, the increase in foreign tourists, and the beginnings of a substantial movement of young Chinese abroad for study. China's relative technological backwardness in almost all fields may be its greatest single economic problem, but the cure inevitably involves, first, recognizing this (as the Chinese have now belatedly done), and second, importing increasing amounts of foreign technology, goods, and technicians. This is bound to stimulate additional pressures among Chinese for a larger share in the consumer benefits which technology can, and indeed is ultimately designed to, deliver. These are all necessarily bourgeois—i.e., urban—trends, values, and results. They will contribute to urban elitism, concentrated on self-advancement in consumerist terms rather than on "serving the people", and will thus abort one of the most basic, and most appealing, goals of the Maoist revolutionary vision. At the same time, they will widen, probably irreparably, the gap between city and countryside, which the Maoist prescription was dedicated to closing.

There is still heavy control over urban populations, and relatively little opportunity for softening or circumventing controls through personal or family connections, as in the rural areas, where most officials are local people. Urban people, who usually, as in most cities anywhere, know their neighbors only on an acquaintance basis if at all and have few kin connections locally, are more reluctant to complain, to speak frankly, or to try through group action, clandestine or otherwise, to evade controls or to develop access to "back doors". Official policy presses for a minimum marriage age of 28 for males and 26 for females (an obvious and effective means of lowering the birth rate). In the cities this is enforced through manipulating work and housing assignments and through group pressures, as is the official norm of no more than two offspring per couple. These policies, however desirable to the national interest, may impose severe personal hardship. In the rural areas, average age at marriage is significantly lower; most rural marriages are still arranged, include a bride price, and are elaborately celebrated in traditional style, all practices explicitly discouraged by the state. Numbers of offspring per couple are also greater than in the cities. It seems clear that traditional social networks can soften controls and circumvent what are seen as undesirable policies. Urban marriages are usually not arranged and are celebrated in the simplest civil ceremony. There are few routes around the relative barrenness of cultural life in the cities. But despite controls and official efforts at austerity, the cities are where most people seem to want to be, given the chance. It is discouraging, but understandable.

There remains a basic conflict between a China bent on increasing production and living standards, and a China committed to austere and self-denying revolutionary ideals, with an inherited anti-urban component. Production and living standards are indeed increasing, but consumption levels are not increasing equally for everyone. Even if they could be made to do so, there is little reason to think that the Chinese, despite the inspiration of

Maoist ideals, are immune to the blandishments of consumerism, any more than many of them have appeared able to resist the attractions of the city and its bourgeois rewards. The Chinese revolution aimed to destroy the city, and then to re-mold it. Instead it appears that the city threatens to destroy the revolution.

China is not unusual in cherishing a sentimental attachment to a rural ideal. Most already industrialized and highly urbanized countries, from Europe through Japan to the United States, retain a wistful *recherche du temps perdu*. The vision of the good society represented, for example, by Thomas Jefferson, with its mistrust of cities and factories and its faith in rural virtues, is still seen by many as a better world. But whatever some individuals may choose as personal life styles, the industrialized countries as a whole have left the Jeffersonian ideal behind them, perhaps with regret but with a feeling of inevitability. And for all who would argue that things were better for most people in a rural pre-industrial era (or are so now in the developing world), one must point to living and working conditions, diet, disease and death rates, and life expectancy as basic measures of well being which destroy the illusion of a rural pre-industrial paradise in any part of the world. Spiritual values, however they may be defined, are doubtless important, but are hard to give priority over simple survival, and conditions of life and work, which have been enhanced by the growth of urban-based industrialization, whatever the psychic or aesthetic costs. Few people would choose to forego the use of anesthesia or vaccination, for example, or to readjust their life styles to exclude all goods and services dependent on fabricated metals (including the transport which makes them accessible).

These and other universally desired advantages can come only as a result of industrialization, practically all of it urban-based and hence accompanied by massive urbanization. Unfortunately, since the package is a mixture of benefits and losses, it does tend to be a package from which it is difficult or impossible to pick and choose. However much individuals or countries may wish to exclude from the package what are seen as undesirables, in practice they must simply be lived with, as a necessary price for the benefits. Economic growth flourishes best on the basis of cost efficiency; hence undesirables which are cheap and efficient, however nasty, such as plastics. But perhaps the hardest undesirable to accept as part of the industrialization package is the city itself, aesthetically ugly, spiritually deadening, environmentally destructive, and seemingly destructive also of most basic human values, except for consumerism. China has seemed to have the best chance of escaping from this dreary scenario, partly because its development is still in the early stages, partly because of its declared intentions. Now one is inclined to wonder.

Results and trends in China thus far do not suggest that its future development pattern will be basically different from that followed by industrializing countries elsewhere since the eighteenth century, despite the problems and human costs involved in that pattern which have helped stimulate the Chinese to seek an alternative path. Urban concentration seems there to stay, and the rural alternative to it as a major component of industrialization does not seem likely to become more than a token gesture. But this does not mean that Chinese cities will soon or even ultimately become like those in the West or Japan. The Maoist vision has made a deep and lasting impact on China. Even as revolutionary ardor cools, as Mao and the early revolutionary struggles recede into history, the legacy of his vision will continue to shape Chinese development policy and action in a way which seems certain to keep it distinctive, including the role of its cities and their structure and nature. Despite Mao's ringing words, the Chinese people are not "blank"; poor, yes, but also the inheritors both of a long imperial tradition and of a now equally powerful revolutionary experience. Mao himself was responsible for drawing beautiful new pictures on that sheet of paper, visions and values which will never be entirely erased or obscured.

The long traditional Chinese emphasis on, even instinct for, spatial planning, as old as Chinese civilization and in sharp contrast with most other cultures, where growth has been comparatively unplanned or haphazard, will also continue to influence especially what happens to and in China's cities. They were in the past the chief foci of the imperial design, with their uniformly planned walls, gates, and avenues; symbolic affirmations of the power and majesty of the state and bearing its imprint both in their planned structure and in the tight controls imposed on them. Their chief role as defenders, supporters, and servants of the rural areas around them, and their location in conformity with population patterns around the country as a whole, each city near the center of its county, also agrees with the Maoist formula. These characteristics of cities and their planned nature have thus been reinforced. Their modern equivalents, from re-planned Peking with its new-and-old monumental buildings and broad avenues, to newly-planned Chengchow or Ta-Ch'ing, to the new smaller cities growing up in every province, will remain distinctively Chinese, and distinctively Peoples' Republic. Perhaps they can continue to be kept freer of uncontrolled overcrowding, slums, violence—and pollution?—than cities elsewhere. Perhaps they can also generate less greed, selfishness, consumerism, and de-humanization?

Whatever the answers, the city has clearly won out as the chief basis of the Chinese development effort. The problems which it generates will be handled in a distinctively Chinese way, but there are no easy or perfect solutions to any human dilemmas. One suspects that the consequences of growing urbanism will be the most difficult of all problems which the Chinese will face in the future as they try to combine revolutionary ideological goals with the drive for industrialization and technological modernization. It is a long way from Yenan, China's Valley Forge as the revolutionary capital in the 1930's and 1940's, and the "Yenan Way", to Peking in the 1980's, with its large industrial complex and its showplace role as the capital of a modernizing country. As Mao put it poignantly in a poem to the dying[60] Chou En-lai, his old revolutionary comrade, written in 1975, not long before his own death in September of 1976:

Loyal parents who sacrificed so much for the nation
Never feared the ultimate fate.
Now that the country has become Red,
Who will be its guardians?

Our mission, unfinished, may take a thousand years;
The struggle tires us, and our hair is gray.
You and I, old friend,
Can we just watch our efforts being washed away?[61]

Even a hundred years is a long time to try to see into the future, but Mao here may be unnecessarily pessimistic, even though understandably so for an aged, sick, and tired revolutionary who sees signs of the old fire dying around him as he prepares for his own death. Rather than his and his colleagues' efforts being washed away, it seems more likely that Mao will be remembered a hundred years from now as one of the truly towering figures of the twentieth century world, one who left it, and especially China, dramatically changed as a result of his efforts and of his vision. The appeal of his radical ideal, and of his formula for people-centered development, will continue to attract support, and above all in China. One can also argue that the Maoist strategy of basing industrialization in the countryside, limiting the growth of cities, and re-making the nature of those that remained, has never really been tried on a thoroughgoing and consistent basis. Indeed, as pointed out, Mao himself was inconsistent at different times and even advocated a renewed emphasis on urban-centered industrialization. Any alternative strategy, necessarily strange and untried, needs time to work out effectively, time for trial and error, and time to demonstrate its virtues and shortcomings in terms of accomplishments, comparative costs, and net benefits. That kind of time even a revolutionary China has not given, or perhaps has not felt it could afford to give under the pressures of the need for rapid economic growth. Perhaps as a somewhat less precarious economic margin can be built up—in China, in India, or elsewhere—an alternative road to development, one which focusses on the rural areas and minimizes the problems associated with big city growth, will be given a full and fair trial. This would need to be over the kind of time period and with the kind of full and consistent support which might produce more conclusive results than we have so far from either the Chinese or the Indian experience. If such a trial is made—as one hopes it might be, in the interests of all of us—it will clearly owe an enormous debt not merely to the original Maoist vision but to the Chinese effort since 1949, however incomplete, to put at least some of it into practice.

Notes

1. A few figures: The Indonesian census of 1970 classifies 60 per cent of the housing stock of Djakarta (population about four and a half million) as "temporary"—i.e., squatter huts; only 8 per cent of all households in Djakarta in 1970 had both electricity and running water, and over 80 per cent of all households were beyond the reach of even basic services. About one third of the residents of Rangoon still live in squatter huts, of which only about a quarter have piped drinking water *or* electricity. Djakarta and Rangoon are probably extreme cases, and suffer from central government ineffectiveness as well as from very slow economic growth rates, but they illustrate typical and widespread problems.

2. From several accounts, as collected in E.R. Pike, *Hard Times: Human Documents of the Industrial Revolution*, New York: Praeger, 1966, pp. 49, 310, 61.

3. See, among many accounts, D.T. Lynch, *Boss Tweed*, New York: Boni and Liveright, 1927.

4. However, see p. 73, for a 1979 "official" figure.

5. In Lu Tzu-chun, compiler, *Ch'ao-lien hsiang-chih* (Village gazetteer of Ch'ao-lien (Kwangtung), statement attributed to Ku Yen-wu (1616–1682). Hong Kong, Lü-kuang Hsin-hui Ch'ao-lien t'ung-hsiang hui, 1954, p. 54.

6. A. Little, *Gleanings from Fifty Years in China*, London, 1910, pp. 29 ff.

7. J.H. Wilson, *China: Travels and Investigations in the Middle Kingdom*, New York, 1887, pp. 21–22.

8. Herman Mast, "Tai Chi-t'ao, Sunism, and Marxism During the May Fourth Movement in Shanghai", *Modern Asian Studies*, 5 (1971), p. 229.

9. Lin Piao (*Linbiao*), "Long Live the Victory of Peoples' War", as published in *Peking Review*, No. 36 (Sept. 3, 1965), pp. 9–30. Lin is quoting here from Mao's *The Chinese Revolution and the Chinese Communist Party*, written in 1939.

10. This is the final stanza of Mao's poem, "Reply to Kuo Mo-jo", dated February 5, 1963, as translated in *China Reconstructs*, Vol. 16 (March, 1967), p. 2.

11. Mao Tse-tung, in *Hung Ch'i* (Red Flag), June 1, 1958, pp. 3–4.

12. For a careful effort at estimation, see E. Onoye, "Regional Distribution of Urban Population in China", *The Developing Economies*, 8 (1970), pp. 92–112.

13. For further discussion and data on this problem, see Christopher Howe, *Urban Employment and Economic Growth in Communist China, 1949–1957*, Cambridge University Press, 1971; Lynn White, "Deviance, Modernization, Rations, and Household Registers in Urban China", in R.W. Wilson, S. Greenblatt, and A.A. Wilson, eds., *Social Control and Deviance in China*, Praeger, 1977, pp. 151–72; Lynn White, "Population and Capital Policies in Chinese Communist Cities", unpublished ms., 1978—and the variety of accounts in the Chinese press cited in all of the above.

14. See Onoye, *op. cit.*

15. The figure of 20 million is given in J.S. Aird, "Population Growth and Distribution in Mainland China", in *An Economic Profile of Mainland China*, Washington: Govt. Printing Office, 1967, p. 382; however, as Aird mentions, this figure is one quoted by foreign journalists and was never officially used.

16. Given in *Ta Kung Pao*, Hong Kong, January 15, 1964.

17. The figures are provided in J.P. Emerson, *Non-Agricultural Employment in Mainland China, 1949–58*, Washington: Govt. Printing Office, 1965, p. 128.

18. Quoted in Stuart Schram, ed., *Mao Tse-tung Unrehearsed—Talks and Letters 1956–1971*, Middlesex: Penguin Books, 1974, pp. 65–67. Chinese text in Huang Ting, ed., *Addenda to the Selected Works of Mao*, Vol. 3: 1949–1959, Peking, 1971, pp. 75–91.

19. The figures are given in N. Lardy, "Economic Planning in the P.R.C.: Central-Provincial Fiscal Relations", in *China: A Reassessment of the Economy*, Washington, 1975, pp. 91–115.

20. See the table on p. 97 of Lardy, *op. cit.*

21. For further details, see N. Lardy, "Centralization and Decentralization in China's Fiscal Management", *China Quarterly*, 61 (March 1975).

22. For further discussion see T.P. Bernstein, *Up to the Mountains and Down to the Villages: The Transfer of Youth from Urban to Rural China*, Yale University Press, 1977; Christopher Howe, ed., *The Development of Shanghai Since 1949*, Cambridge University Press, 1980.

23. For more detail, see Leo Orleans, *Every Fifth Child: The Population of China*, Stanford University Press, 1972; and *ibid.*, *China's Birth Rate, Death Rate, and Population Growth: Another Perspective*, U.S. Government Printing Office, Washington, D.C., 1977.

24. See C.R. Roll and K.C. Yeh, "Balance in Coastal and Inland Industrial Development", in *China: A Reassessment (op. cit)*, pp. 81–93.

25. The above and following discussion of small-scale industry, including figures cited, is based on Carl Riskin, "China's Rural Industries: Self-Reliant Systems or Independent Kingdoms?", *China Quarterly*, 73 (March, 1978), pp. 77–98; John Sigurdson, *Rural Industrialization in China*, Harvard University Press, 1977; D. Perkins, ed., *Rural Small Scale Industry in the Peoples' Republic of China*, California University Press, 1977 (the report of the U.S. delegation in 1975); and accounts in the Chinese press, including those cited in the foregoing works.

26. J. Sigurdson, "Rural Industry and the Internal Transfer of Technology", in S. Schram, *Authority, Participation, and Cultural Change in China*, Cambridge University Press, 1973, p. 208.

27. For a valuable general discussion and analysis of this problem, see E.A.J. Johnson, *The Organization of Space in Developing Countries*, M.I.T. Press, 1970.

28. However, Chinese press reports in 1977 gave 1.7 million as the population of Chengchow—a good example of the statistical problems China presents. It is likely that the lower figures refer only to the compact urbanized area and the higher ones to a larger administrative area which includes rural-agricultural land and population, as with most Chinese cities. Unfortunately, we just do not know; but see Table I on page 81.

29. See D. Perkins, ed., *Rural Small Scale Industry (op. cit.)*, Chapter 9.

30. As reported by Hsin Hua (*Xin Hua*) News Agency, June 28, 1979, p. 12.

31. For relevant official documents, see H.Y. Tien, *China's Population Struggle*, Ohio State Univeristy Press, 1973, Appendix D. Tien's book is also a useful general discussion of the population problem and of the available data.

32. For further discussion of this problem, see S.D. Chang, "The Changing System of Chinese Cities", *Annals of the Association of American Geographers*, 66 (September, 1976), pp. 398-415.

33. "The New Shanghai in Socialist Construction", *Ch'eng-shih chien-she* (Urban Construction), Vol. 10 (October, 1975), pp. 28-31, as translated in Joint Publications Research Service, Washington, D.C., No. 5258, "Urban Construction in Communist China", Part II, August, 1960, p. 42.

34. For a fictional but plausible and vivid picture of the less appealing human aspects of urban life under this system of control during the Cultural Revolution and its aftermath—admittedly an especially difficult period—see Chen Jo-hsi, *The Execution of Mayor Yin*, Indiana University Press, 1978, a collection of human-interest stories by a Chinese writer who lived there from 1966 until she emigrated to Canada in 1973.

35. As summarized from Chinese press reports of the early 1970's in C.L. Salter, "Chinese Experiments in Urban Space: The Quest for an Agrapolitan China", *Habitat*, Vol. 4 (1976), pp. 19-35.

36. As one example, see "Multi-Purpose Use: Important Policy for Industrial Production", *Peking Review*, 14 (February 5, 1971), which suggests, as do other articles in the Chinese press, that the imminent collapse of capitalism may result as much from its destructive impact on the environment as from other inherent flaws.

37. For some descriptive, and generally uncritical, accounts of Ta Ch'ing, see the official publication *Taching; Red Banner on China's Industrial Front*, Peking: Foreign Languages Press, 1972; and Leslie W. Chan, *Ta Ch'ing: A Maoist Model for Economic Development*, Canberra: Australian National University Press, 1974.

38. See *inter alia* D. Lampton, "Administration of the Pharmaceutical, Research, Public Health, and Population Bureaucracies", *China Quarterly*, 74 (Junc, 1978), pp. 385-400.

39. For more detail, see R.W. Lee, "The Hsia-Fang System: Marxism and Modernization," *China Quarterly*, No. 28 (Oct.-Dec. 1966) pp. 40-62.

40. T.P. Bernstein has published a book-length study of this movement, *Up to the Mountains and Down to the Villages: The Transfer of Youth from Urban to Rural China*, Yale University Press, 1977; P.J. Seybolt, ed., *The Rustication of Urban Youth in China: A Social Experiment*, White Plains, N.Y.: M.E. Sharpe, 1977, is primarily a

translation of a Chinese compilation published in 1973 of articles which appeared in the Chinese press at the time of an investigation of the program and the adoption of some remedial measures, plus other Chinese articles on selection and adjustment of urban youth in rural areas published between 1973 and 1976. Additional data and analysis are provided by Chen Pi-chao, "Over-urbanization, Rustication of Urban-educated Youths, and the Politics of Rural Transformation," *Comparative Politics*, 4 (April, 1972), pp. 361–86, and by Martin Singer, *The Revolutionization of Youth in the P.R.C.*, Ph.D. thesis, University of Michigan, 1977.

41. For a fascinating semi-fictional account of this period by a supposed ex-Red Guard, see Ken Ling (pseudonym), *The Revenge of Heaven*, New York: Putnam, 1972.

42. T.P. Bernstein, *op. cit.*

43. See P.J. Seybolt, *op. cit.*

44. See *Chieh-fang Jih-pao* (Liberation Daily), February 7, 1979, as reported also by Agence France Presse in Peking on February 10.

45. As reported by Agence France Presse, Peking, April 22, 1979.

46. Information on education obtained through personal observation and interviews and through communication from a number of recent (1979) visitors to China, especially my colleague D.J. Munro, who had extensive talks with a variety of officials and teachers in the education system.

47. For a study of wage and salary rates, see Christopher Howe, *Employment and Economic Growth in Urban China, 1949–1957*, Cambridge University Press, 1971.

48. As perhaps the best samples of this literature, see Subramian Swamy, *Economic Growth in China and India, 1952–1970*, Chicago University Press, 1973, and S. Swamy, "The Economic Distance Between China and India, 1955–1973," *China Quarterly*, 70 (June, 1977), pp. 371–81.

49. Traditional Chinese agriculture was also more intensive and more productive per acre than in India. As with industrialization, it is easier to double or triple a low output than a high one, and harder to improve an already developed system than a less developed one—a perverse kind of advantage for India after 1947, and a disadvantage for China.

50. On the Chinese health system, see David Lampton, "Performance and the Chinese Political System: A Preliminary Assessment of Health and Education Policies," *China Quarterly*, 75 (September 1978), pp. 509–39; and *ibid.*, *The Politics of Medicine in China*, Boulder: Westview Press, 1977.

51. Much of the material here is based on personal observation and conversations with officials, planners, scholars, and local people in the course of a two-month tour of urban and rural India by car in late 1978, followed by a briefer return tour of urban and rural China in 1979.

52. See Lampton, *op. cit.*, and P.J. Seybolt, *Revolutionary Education in China*, New York, 1973.

53. As mentioned in Chapter 6, it now seems that major changes have been taking place in the Chinese education system since about 1977, designed to correct these problems.

54. M.K. Gandhi in *The Harijan* (a paper which he founded), August 29, 1936.

55. From Gandhi's speeches in 1946 as quoted in R. Mayur, ed., *A Profile of Urbanization*, Delhi: National Society of Urban Development, 1978, p. 14.

56. For further discussion, see R. Murphey, "City and Countryside as Ideological Issues: India and China," *Comparative Studies in Society and History*, 14 (June, 1972), pp. 250–67; R. Murphey, "The Urban Road to Development," Lee, N., Leung, C.K., eds., *China: Development and Challenge*, Hong Kong University Press, 1979, pp. 217–232.

57. For samples of the extensive literature on Indian planning and development, see K.V. Sundaram, *Urban and Regional Planning in India*, Delhi: Vikas, 1977; R.P. Misra, K.V. Sundaram, and V.L.S. Prakasa Rao, *Regional Development and Planning in India*, Delhi: Vikas, 1974; Bepin Bihari, *Rural Industrialization in India*, Delhi: Vikas, 1976.

58. From the official text of Hua's Report, as published in English, in *Peking Review*, No. 10, March 10, 1978.

59. Hua's statement to U.N. Secretary-General Waldheim, as reported by UPI in Peking.

60. Chou died in January, 1976.

61. The poem is most conveniently found in Maurice Meisner, *Mao's China: A History of the Peoples' Republic*, Free Press, New York, 1977, pp. 380–81.

Bibliography

Abu-Lughod, J. and Hay, R., eds., *Third World Urbanization*, New York: Methuen, 1971.

Aird, J.S., "Population Growth and Distribution in Mainland China", *An Economic Profile of Mainland China*, Joint Economic Committee of the U.S. Congress, Washington, 1967, pp. 341-401.

Andors, Stephen, *China's Industrial Development*, New York: Pantheon, 1977.

Andors, Stephen, "Urbanization and Urban Government in China's Development", *Economic Development and Cultural Change*, 26 (1978), pp. 526-46.

Bernstein, T.P., *Up to the Mountains and Down to the Villages: The Transfer of Youth From Urban to Rural China*, New Haven: Yale University Press, 1977.

Bernstein, T.P., "Urban Youth in the Countryside: Problems of Adaptation and Remedies", *China Quarterly*, 69 (March, 1977), pp. 75-108.

Bettelheim, Charles, *China's Cultural Revolution and Industrial Organization in China*, New York: Monthly Review Press, 1974.

Bihari, Bepin, *Rural Industrialization in India*, Delhi: Vikas, 1976.

Blecher, Marc, "Income Distribution in Small Rural Chinese Communities", *China Quarterly*, 68 (December, 1976), pp. 797-816.

Breese, Gerald, ed., *Urbanization in Newly Developing Countries*, Englewood Cliffs, N.J.: Prentice-Hall, 1969.

Brutzkus, E., "Centralized v. Decentralized Patterns of Urbanization in Developing Countries", *Economic Development and Cultural Change*, 23 (1975), pp. 633–652.

Buck, David, "Directions in Chinese Urban Planning", *Urbanism Past and Present*, 1 (1976), pp. 24–35.

Buck, David, *Urban Change in China*, Madison: University of Wisconsin Press, 1978.

Buttler, R., *Growth Role Theory and Economic Development*, Lexington, Mass.: Lexington Books, 1975.

Carin, Robert, *Power Industry in Communist China*, Hong Kong: Union Research Institute, 1969.

Chan, Leslie W., *Ta Ch'ing: A Maoist Model for Economic Development*, Canberra: Australian National University Press, 1974.

Chang, S.D., "The Changing System of Chinese Cities", *Annals of the Association of American Geographers*, 66 (1976), pp. 398–415.

Chang, S.D., "The Historical Trend of Chinese Urbanization", *Annals of the Association of American Geographers*, 53 (1963), pp. 109–43.

Chang, S.D., "Some Observations on the Morphology of Chinese Walled Cities", *Annals of the Association of American Geographers*, 60 (1970), pp. 63–91.

Chen, C.S., "Population Growth and Urbanization in China, 1953–1970", *Geographical Review*, 63(1973), pp. 55–72.

Chen Jo-hsi, *The Execution of Mayor Yin*, Bloomington: Indiana University Press, 1978.

Chen Pi-chao, "Over-urbanization, Rustication of Urban-educated Youths, and the Role of Rural Transformation", *Comparative Politics*, 4 (1972), pp. 361–86.

Crook, F.W., "The Commune System in the Peoples' Republic of China, 1973–74", *China: A Reassessment of the Economy*, Joint Economic Committee of the U.S. Congress, Washington, 1975, pp. 366–410.

Donnithorne, Audrey, "China's Cellular Economy: Some Economic Trends Since the Cultural Revolution", *China Quarterly*, 52 (December 1972), pp. 605–19.

Dwyer, D.J., ed., *The City in the Third World*, New York: Barnes and Noble, 1974.

Eberhard, Wolfram, "Data on the Structure of the Chinese City in the Pre-industrial Period", *Economic Development and Cultural Change*, 4 (1955), pp. 253–68.

Elvin, Mark, and Skinner, G.W., eds., *The Chinese City Between Two Worlds*, Stanford, Calif.: Stanford University Press, 1974.

Emerson, J.P., *Non-agricultural Employment in Mainland China, 1947–1958*, Washington: Government Printing Office, 1965.

Field, R.M., Lardy, N., and Emerson, J.P., "Industrial Output by Province in China, 1949–1973", *China Quarterly*, 63 (September, 1975), pp. 409–34.

Fisher, J.C., "Planning the City of Socialist Man", *Journal of the American Institute of Planners*, 28 (1962), pp. 251–65.

Foreign Languages Press, *Taching: Red Banner on China's Industrial Front*, Peking, 1972.

Gurley, J.G., *China's Economy and the Maoist Strategy*, New York: Monthly Review Press, 1976.

Gurley, J.G., "Rural Development in China, 1949–1972 and the Lessons to be Learned From It", *World Development*, 3 (1975), pp. 455–71.

Howe, Christopher, ed., *The Development of Shanghai Since 1949*, Cambridge and New York: Cambridge University Press, 1980.

Howe, Christopher, *Urban Employment and Economic Growth in Communist China, 1949–1957*, Cambridge and New York: Cambridge University Press, 1971.

Howe, Christopher, *Wage Patterns and Wage Policy in Modern China*, Cambridge and New York: Cambridge University Press, 1973.

Hu Chang-tu, *Aspects of Chinese Education*, New York: Columbia University Press, 1969.

Ishikawa, Shigeru, "Choice of Techniques in Mainland China", *The Developing Economies*, Tokyo, (September–December, 1962), pp. 24–56.

Ivory, P.E. and Lavely, W.R., "Rustication, Demographic Change, and Development in Shanghai", *Asian Quarterly*, 17 (1977), pp. 440–55.

Joint Economic Committee of the U.S. Congress, *China: A Reassessment of the Economy*, Washington, 1975.

Johnson, E.A.J., *The Organization of Space in Developing Countries*, Cambridge, Mass.: M.I.T. Press, 1970.

Koshizawa, Akira, "China's Urban Planning: Toward Development Without Urbanization", *The Developing Economies*, Tokyo, 16 (1978), pp. 3–33.

Lampton, David, "Performance and the Chinese Political System: A Preliminary Assessment of Education and Health Policies", *China Quarterly*, 75 (September, 1978), pp. 509–39.

Lampton, David, *The Politics of Medicine in China*, Boulder, Colorado: Westview Press, 1977.

Lardy, Nicholas, "Centralization and Decentralization in China's Fiscal Management", *China Quarterly*, 61 (March, 1975), pp. 25–60.

Lee, Hong-yung, "Mao's Strategy for Revolutionary Change", *China Quarterly*, 77 (March, 1979), pp. 50–73.

Lee, R.W., "The Hsia-fang System: Marxism and Modernization", *China Quarterly*, 28 (December, 1966), pp. 40–62.

Lewis, J.W., ed., *The City in Communist China*, Stanford, Calif.: Stanford University Press, 1971.

Ling, Ken (pseudonym), *The Revenge of Heaven*, New York: Putnam, 1972.

Lo, C.P., Pannell, C.W., and Welch, R., "Land Use Changes and City Planning in Shenyang and Canton", *Geographical Review*, 67 (1977), pp. 268–83.

Lowenthal, Richard, "Development vs. Utopia in Communist Policy", in C. Johnson, ed., *Change in Communist Systems*, Stanford, Calif.: Stanford University Press, 1970, pp. 33–116.

Ma, L.J.C., "The Chinese Approach to City Planning", *Asian Survey*, 19 (September 1979), pp. 838–855.

Mayur, R., ed., *A Profile of Urbanization*, Delhi: National Society of Urban Development, 1978.

McGee, T.G., *The Urbanization Process in the Third World*, London: Bell, 1971.

Meisner, Maurice, *Mao's China: A History of the Peoples' Republic*, New York: Free Press, 1977.

Misra, R.P., *Million Cities of India*, Delhi: Vikas, 1978.

Misra, R.P., Rao, V.L.S.P., and Sundaram, K.V., *Regional Development and Planning in India*, Delhi: Vikas, 1974.

Mote, F., "The City in Traditional Chinese Civilization", in Liu, James T.C., and Tu, W.M., eds., *Traditional China*, Englewood Cliffs, N.J.: Prentice Hall, 1970, pp. 42–49.

Murphey, R., "Chinese Urbanization Under Mao", in B. Berry, ed., *Urbanization and Counter-urbanization*, Beverly Hills, Calif.: Sage Publications, 1976, pp. 311–31.

Murphey, R., "The City as a Center of Change: Western Europe and China", *Annals of the Association of American Geographers*, 44 (1954), pp. 349–62.

Murphey, R., "City and Countryside as Ideological Issues: India and China", *Comparative Studies in Society and History*, 14 (1972), pp. 250–67.

Murphey, R., "City and Society in China", *Michigan Quarterly*, 17 (1978), pp. 176–94.

Murphey, R., *The Outsiders: The Western Experience in India and China*, Ann Arbor: University of Michigan Press, 1977.

Murphey, R., *Shanghai: Key to Modern China*, Cambridge, Mass.: Harvard University Press, 1953.

Murphey, R., "Traditionalism and Colonialism: Changing Urban Roles in Asia", *Journal of Asian Studies*, 29 (1969), pp. 67–84.

Murphey, R., "The Treaty Ports and China's Modernization", in Elvin, M., and Skinner, G.W., eds., *The Chinese City Between Two Worlds*, Stanford, Calif.: Stanford University Press, 1974, pp. 17–72.

Murphey, R., "The Urban Road to Development", in Lee, N., and Leung, C.K., eds., *China: Development and Challenge*, Hong Kong University Press, 1979, pp. 217–232.

Onoye, Etsuzo, "Regional Distribution of Urban Population in

China", *The Developing Economies*, Tokyo, 8 (1970), pp. 93-107.

Orleans, Leo, *China's Birth Rate, Death Rate, and Population Growth: Another Perspective*, Washington: U.S. Government Printing Office, 1977.

Orleans, Leo, *Every Fifth Child: The Population of China*, Stanford, Calif: Stanford University Press, 1972.

Pannell, C.W., "Past and Present City Structure in China", *Town Planning Review*, 48 (1977), pp. 157-72.

Perkins, Dwight, ed., *China's Modern Economy in Historical Perspective*, Stanford, Calif: Stanford University Press, 1975.

Perkins, Dwight, ed., *Rural Small Scale Industry in the Peoples' Republic of China*, Berkeley: University of California Press, 1977.

Qadeer, M.A., "Do Cities 'Modernize' Developing Countries?", *Comparative Studies in Society and History*, 16 (1974), pp. 266-83.

Rice, Edgar, *Mao's Way*, Berkeley: University of California Press, 1972.

Richman, Barry, *Industrial Society in Communist China*, New York: Random House, 1969.

Riskin, Carl, "China's Rural Industries: Self-reliant Systems or Independent Kingdoms?", *China Quarterly*, 73 (March, 1978), pp. 77-98.

Riskin, Carl, "Rural Industrialization in China: Approaches and Results", *World Development*, 3 (1975), pp. 527-38.

Riskin, Carl, "Small Industry and the Chinese Model of Development", *China Quarterly*, 46 (June, 1971), pp. 245-73.

Roll, C.R. and Yeh, K.C., "Balance in Coastal and Inland Industrial Development", in *China: A Reassessment of the Economy*, Washington, 1975, pp. 81-93.

Rozman, Gilbert, *Urban Networks in Ch'ing China and Tokugawa Japan*, Princeton, N.J.: Princeton University Press, 1973.

Salaff, Janet, "The Urban Communes and Anti-city Experiment in Communist China", *China Quarterly*, 29 (March, 1967), pp. 82-110.

Salter, C.L., "Chinese Experiments in Urban Space: The Quest for an Agrapolitan China", *Habitat*, 4 (1976), pp. 19-35.

Selden, Mark, *The Yenan Way in Revolutionary China*, Cambridge, Mass.: Harvard University Press, 1971.

Seybolt, P.J., *Revolutionary Education in China*, White Plains, New York: International Arts and Sciences Press, 1973.

Seybolt, P.J., ed., *The Rustication of Urban Youth in China: A Social Experiment*, White Plains, New York: M.E. Sharpe, 1977.

Shirk, Susan, "Educational Reform and Political Backlash: Recent Changes in Chinese Educational Policy", *Comparative Education Review*, 23 (1979), pp. 183-217.

Sigurdson, Jon, *Rural Industrialization in China*, Cambridge, Mass.: Harvard University Press, 1977.

Sigurdson, Jon, "Rural Industry and the Internal Transfer of Technology", in Stuart Schram, ed., *Authority, Participation, and Cultural Change in China*, Cambridge and New York: Cambridge University Press, 1973.

Skinner, G.W., ed., *The City in Late Traditional China*, Stanford, Calif: Stanford University Press, 1977.

Smil, Vaclav, and Kuz, T., "China: A Quantitative Comparison of Development, 1950–1970", *Economic Development and Cultural Change*, 27 (1979), pp. 653–668.

Sundaram, K.V., *Urban and Regional Planning in India*, Delhi: Vikas, 1977.

Survey of the China Mainland Press, U.S. Consulate-General, Hong Kong (periodical).

Swamy, Subramian, "The Economic Distance Between China and India, 1955–1973", *China Quarterly*, 70 (June, 1977), pp. 371–81.

Swamy, Subramian, *Economic Growth in China and India, 1952–1970*, Chicago: University of Chicago Press, 1973.

Terrill, Ross, *Flowers on an Iron Tree: Five Cities of China*, Boston: Little Brown, 1975.

Tien, H.Y., *China's Population Struggle*, Columbus: Ohio State University Press, 1973.

Towers, G., "City Planning in China", *Journal of the Royal Town Planning Institute*, 59 (1973), pp. 125–27.

Ullman, M.B., *Cities of Mainland China, 1953 and 1958*, Washington: U.S. Government Printing Office, 1961.

Vogel, Ezra, *Canton Under Communism*, Cambridge, Mass.: Harvard University Press, 1969.

Wheelwright, E.L. and Goodstadt, L., *China's Search for Plenty: The Economics of Mao Tse-tung*, New York: Weatherhill, 1973.

Wheelwright, E.L., and McFarlane, B., *The Chinese Road to Socialism*, New York: Monthly Review Press, 1970.

White, Lynn T., *Careers in Shanghai*, Berkeley: University of California Press, 1978.

White, Lynn T., "Deviance, Modernization, Rationing, and Household Registers in Urban China", in Wilson, R.W., Greenblatt, S., and Wilson, A.A., eds., *Social Control and Deviance in China*, New York: Praeger, 1977, pp. 151–72.

White, Lynn T., "Low Power: Small Enterprises in Shanghai, 1949–1967", *China Quarterly*, 73 (March, 1978), pp. 45–76.

White, Lynn T., "Population and Capital Policies in Chinese Communist Cities", unpublished manuscript, 1978.

Yajima, Kinji, "Communist China's Economic Modernization Program", *Issues and Studies*, 14 (1978), pp. 37–52.

Yu, C.L., "Local Industry and its Impact on Agricultural Development in China", *Asia Quarterly*, 4 (1971), pp. 32–42.

Index